Collectibles

Collectibles

Nancy Dunnan

SILVER BURDETT PRESS

Published by Silver Burdett Press, Inc., a division of Simon & Schuster, Inc., Prentice Hall Bldg., Englewood Cliffs, NJ 07632.

Created and produced by: Blackbirch Graphics, Inc.

Project Editor: Emily Easton
Designer: Cynthia Minichino

Manufactured in the United States of America

10 9 8 7 6 5 4 3 2 1

Library of Congress Cataloging-in-Publication Data
Dunnan, Nancy.
 Collectibles/Nancy Dunnan
 (The Inside Track Library)
 Includes index.
 0-382-24029-4 paper
 1. Antiques—Handbooks, manuals, etc. I. Title. II. Series:
Dunnan, Nancy. Inside Track Library.
NK1125. D786 1990
745.1— dc20
ISBN 0-382-09918-4 LSB
90-40252 CIP

(Frontispiece)
Collecting is a passion that often begins early in life.

CONTENTS

NO SMOKING

FLOUR

Collectibles reflect the culture and taste of earlier days.

1

GETTING STARTED

C ollecting is like eating peanuts—you have one and can't stop," said the late Malcolm S. Forbes, chairman of *Forbes Magazine*. He knew: Forbes acquired 12,000 toy soldiers, 1,200 miniature motorcycles, 40 shipbuilders' models, 500 toy boats, and 12 of the world's most famous and costly collectibles—Fabergé eggs.

What Are Collectibles?

Collectibles are things people purposefully find, buy, and save. They can be traditional items, such as furniture, silver, paintings, stamps, and coins; or collectibles can be more unusual, such as ink wells, Elvis Presley memorabilia, baseball cards, dolls, and fountain pens.

Collectibles must have charm, nostalgic appeal, or artistic merit. They usually are at least 30 years old—the number of years it takes each of us to grow

Antique: An item of value that is at least 100 years old. A semi-antique is 50 years old.

up and become old enough to long for the toys, clothes, furniture, and gadgets of childhood. But you don't have to be out of school to love **antiques** or things that will eventually become antiques. You can start building your collection today and by the time you are 20 or 25, it may be very valuable.

Among the many items that have been collected over the years are arcade and pinball machines, autographs, baseball cards, beer cans, books, bottles, bottle openers, cameras, carousel animals, cigarette lighters, circus memorabilia, clothing, combs, comic books, detective and mystery stories, dime novels, dishes, dolls, embroidery and needle-work, fans, figurines, fishing lures, folk art, furni-ture, greeting cards, inkwells, magazines, medals, menus, movie and theatrical memorabilia, musical instruments, opera mementos, pens and pencils, phonographs, photographs, pipes, political souve-nirs, postcards, radios, religious items, sheet music, silver, telephones, and World's Fair souvenirs.

Collectibles represent many facets of society: its technology, its artistic ability, and even its desire to be entertained.

Collectibles also help preserve and transmit information about our culture that would otherwise be lost. They tell us about ourselves in different eras—what we liked at that time, what we found amusing, and what was historically significant about our past.

Collectibles as an Investment

Some collectibles are "investment grade;" these are considered fine enough to be included in museum collections. An investment-grade collectible is one that is relatively scarce as well as historically and/or artistically important. It is usually in excellent condition.

Collectibles as an investment are **tangible objects.** Their value lies in their physical presence. They do not represent something else, the way a stock represents ownership in a company or a certificate of deposit represents money. Rather, the collectible in and of itself is the object, the thing of value.

Tangible object: Something you can see and feel such as furniture, land, silver, a car, or a painting.

In the financial market, buying and selling stocks and bonds is standardized. Investors know that a certain number of stocks and bonds are always available for trading. Their prices are published every day in the newspaper and they are available through stockbrokers. (See another book in this series, *The Stock Market,* for details.) But the purchase of collectibles is very different, primarily because the market is not standardized and prices are not uniformly published for the public. Some rare items, in fact, are traded only now and then, perhaps once or twice in a decade.

After you read this book and experiment with buying and selling some of the inexpensive collectibles described in Part Two, you may decide to deal in investment-grade items. This requires a great deal of money and expertise, but those who do it well find it extremely rewarding.

Deciding What to Collect

You should collect only those items in which you're really interested. If you love Barbie dolls or movie posters, then that's what you should collect. If you follow the Yankees, Red Sox, and Indians every summer, then baseball cards are a likely choice. If you like to read, then begin collecting **first editions** of your favorite authors. Collecting can be time-consuming and expensive, so you want the hours you devote to it to be fun. Never choose a collectible to impress your friends or because it's very

First edition: Total number of copies first printed from the same type and issued at the same time.

expensive. The primary purpose of collecting is to enjoy what you buy regardless of its price.

For more ideas on what to collect, read the list on pages 16 and 17.

Specializing

After you select one or two broad categories that are personally intriguing, let's say stamps and autographs, then give some thought to specializing. Specializing refers to picking out a particular style, era, artist, or type of collectible within a broad category. For example, if you like to collect stamps, you might decide to focus only on Civil War stamps, or stamps with portraits of famous women on them. Within the category of autographs, you could specialize in signatures of movie stars, politicians, or famous writers.

Specialization makes collecting easier because it helps narrow down the choices and it forces you to spend your time wisely. It is also important financially: all other things being equal, a specialized collection is more valuable than a randomly assembled hodgepodge.

What's Hot When

Talk to any collector and he or she will tell you, "Oh, if I'd only saved my…it would be worth a fortune today!" Determining what items surrounding us now will have value in the future is not easy. But the best barometer for gauging future worth is to consider which items will tell future generations about our life style, our times, and our activities. Also analyze why certain items have become valuable and look for similar factors in contemporary items. Here are some things that just might be worth a lot of money by the year 2000 or 2050:

A "good buy" may one day turn into a valuable antique.

Baseball cards are relatively inexpensive collectibles. They can increase in value dramatically.

• *American furniture.* Although Colonial and Federal pieces are already extremely high in price, Centennial furniture (replicas of Colonial pieces made in 1876) are still affordable. Look for smaller pieces priced under $1,000.

• *Art moderne furniture.* Heavier and darker than the more popular art deco, art moderne pieces are still reasonably priced.

• *Autographs.* Because collectors generally prefer art over history, wonderful bargains in historic autographs cost only a few dollars.

• *Bimillennium.* In anticipation of the observance of the year 2000, a number of bimillenium items are being produced. Look for commemorative coins in bronze, silver, and gold, posters, buttons, etc.

• *Czech Glassware and Goods.* Antiques and crafts from Eastern Europe are expected to gain favor as glasnost heightens America's appreciation of the region. Look for fine bottles, vases, and glasses priced under $200.

• *Fountain pens.* New Mont Blanc or Pelikan pens cost well over $200, but a 1920 pen, in working order, sells for around $100. Look for the top names: Parker, Schaeffer, and Waterman.

• *Lunch boxes.* In the 1970s metal lunch boxes started to be replaced by plastic ones. Today a Jetsons box that sold for $1 at a 1980 garage sale is valued at $200. Look for boxes with the original thermos and stick with popular characters from the 1950s and 1960s TV shows such as the Flintstones, Daniel Boone, and Hopalong Cassidy.

• *Michael Jackson memorabilia.* The singer, whose career began in the late 1960s as part of a family act, the Jackson Five, has continued to capture headlines for his cosmetic surgery, mega-hit albums, and his unusual behavior. Look for original albums, posters, the Michael Jackson doll, buttons, etc.

• *Movie star memorabilia.* Although Marilyn Monroe's red dress from "Gentlemen Prefer Blondes" sold for $12,000, for far less you can collect movie scripts, posters, and costumes.

• *Nixon Watergate memorabilia.* Richard Nixon, because he is the only U.S. president ever to resign from office, is likely to become a focal point of interest for collectors for generations to come. After his death, Nixon memorabilia could take on

IDEAS FOR A SPECIALIZED COLLECTION

Category	Specializations	Category	Specializations
Advertising art	Tin boxes for coffee/tea	Buttons	For children
	Coca-Cola trays		With gemstones
	Soap ads		Brass
		Christmas ornaments	Wooden ones
Automobiles	Pontiacs		Cloth ones
	Convertibles		Animals
	Two-seaters		
		Coins	Commemorative
Autographs	Movie stars		Colonial coins
	Sports heros		Susan B. Anthony
	Politicians		
Baseball cards	One team		
	Players from your state	Comic books	Popeye books
	Rookies		Superman books
			Disney books
Books	First editions		
	Books about a president	Cookie jars	Animals
	Books by one author or illustrator		People
		Dolls	Barbie dolls
			All-cloth
			Boxed dolls
Bottles	Coca-Cola bottles		
	Medicinal bottles	Fountain pens	By a manufacturer
	Pressed glass bottles		Foreign pens

Category	Specializations	Category	Specializations

Jewelry	Art nouveau
	Earrings
	Ceramic
		Pottery and
		porcelain
			By motif:
			  butterflies,
			  corn
			By maker

Maps	Of your state 19th- century maps	Prints	Bird prints By artist
Model trains	For girls Roundhouses	Silver items	Baby spoons Hat pins Thimbles
Movie posters	Silent movies Science fiction James Dean	Tools	Early farm tools Doctor's tools
Phonograph records	Elvis records Beatles records	Watches, clocks	Mickey Mouse Swiss-made

Political
memorabilia
	John F.
	  Kennedy
	  buttons
	A specific
	  election
	Cuff links		

Post cards	Of your state World's Fairs Hotels		

A doll collection makes an interesting display.

even greater value. Look for the Watergate bumper stickers made by the Omnimedia Company of St. Louis which read: "Impeachment with Honor," "Exorcise Nixon," and "Honk If You Think He's Guilty" (priced around $20). Also look for buttons, first edition books, and other related material.

• *Record Albums.* As compact discs take over from vinyl records, the latter will become an endangered species. Vinyl records most worth collecting will be debut albums by groups that went on to become famous. Look for distinctive sleeve cover art, which adds value. Expect to pay around $50 per album.

Another best bet: 45 rpms recorded by little known all-male black harmony groups of the 1950s, such as the Vibranaires and the Larks, on Harlem or Chance labels. Only a few thousand copies were issued, making them a unique collector's item. Also look for: original Elvis Presley and Beatles albums, records by the rhythm and blues vocal group of the 1950s called the Swallows, original albums of musical comedies, such as "Damn Yankees," "My Fair Lady," etc., and older ones, such as Enrico Caruso records. A related collectible is sheet music.

• *Silver.* Both American Colonial and British silver remain affordable—far more so than contemporary silver. Smaller items sell for $250 and less.

• *Star Trek memorabilia.* The most enduring TV show of the 1960s was Star Trek. Since then the popular motion picture series that reunited the original cast of the Starship Enterprise for trips where no man has gone before has kindled new interest in the classic show. Look for any Star Trek collectible—dolls, posters, buttons, autographs, etc.

• *Stone Age computers.* Models from the 1970s such as Osborne, Timex, and Sinclair, selling for

BARBRA STREISAND'S COLLECTION

In 1962, when this famous singer was making only $50 a week performing in little-known cabarets, she could only afford to buy clothes in thrift shops. Yet, whatever money was left over after paying the rent, she spent building a collection of small items—porcelain eggs, cameo brooches, and old jewelry in particular. After Barbra became a Broadway star in 1964, she began collecting finer items, including paintings, museum-

Barbra Streisand

quality furniture and rugs, Gallo sculptures, and Tiffany glass. Today Barbra Streisand has one of the largest private collections of Erté prints, sketches, and silkscreens. According to a close friend, Barbra never throws out anything; when she runs out of room in her house, she simply stores pieces in a warehouse. Experts estimate that her collectibles are worth at least $20 million, not including furs and jewelry!

$100 and more, are appreciating in value. Also look for related items that illustrate the technology's birth—such as the first user's guides, out-of-print books, and tickets to conferences.

• *TV Sets.* This is the era of the couch potato, so it's not surprising that TV sets from the 1940s and 1950s are becoming collector's items. Look for 1940s Stromberg-Carlson, pre-1950 black and white sets, 1951 color (debut year) sets, and sets with unusual designs.

• *Walt Disney celluloids.* These hand-painted transparencies, also called cels, made for Disney's classic animated films, were thrown away in the early days. Today, single frames are appreciating rapidly in value. Cels made before Walt Disney died are more precious than later ones. Prices range from several hundred to several thousand dollars.

An antique dealer may buy or pick up what other people discard.

2

THE HUNT

ollectibles can be found almost anywhere—
in a desk drawer; in the attic; buried in the
basement; as part of an **auction,** garage sale,
or flea market; or from specialized **dealers.**
Here are some of the places to look for treasures.

Auction: A public sale at which objects are held up for bids. The person who bids the most gets the object.

Where to Find Collectibles

At Home
Start your treasure hunt in your own home or that of
your grandparents or an older aunt or uncle. Ask
them to let you look at everything stored in the
basement, garage, or attic. Poke around the shed,
barn, or storage bin. Carefully sort through the
boxes, bureaus, cabinets, drawers, and trunks. And
remind your family not to throw away anything
over 25 years old—that's just the point when some
items start to rise in value and appeal.

Dealer: Someone, usually an expert, who buys or sells a certain kind of collectible.

Thrift Shops and Charity Outlets

These are frequently run by volunteers or others who may be unaware of the value of their inventory. Check the ones in your neighborhood on a regular basis to keep up on new shipments.

Flea Markets

The French claim to have invented the idea of the flea market. Around 1880, ragpickers were banned from the streets of Paris. Subsequently, a brisk trade grew up just outside the city limits. But anything purchased from there was bound to be filled with bugs, hence the name.

Today, flea market sales are conducted all over the country, usually on weekends, and are advertised in local newspapers and publications devoted to collecting. At flea markets, between twenty and several hundred dealers gather together and display an array of collectibles on tables set up for the occasion. They are fun to attend and sometimes you can find what you're looking for at a reasonable price. Dealers that exhibit at flea markets handle a large number of items, for which they pay very little. Because they want to turn over their stock quickly, they often are willing to bargain.

Always arrive early at a flea market, preferably when the first dealers are setting up their tables. An exceptional buy tends to go to the first person who recognizes its value.

Among the best-known American flea markets for collectibles and antiques are:
• *Brimfield, MA:* J&J Promotions Antiques & Collectibles Show. Held three times a year (May, July, September); 413-245-3436. More than 750 dealers participate in these Thursday through Saturday shows.
• *New York, NY:* Annex Antiques Fair & Flea

Market, Avenue of the Americas at 25th Street.
Held Saturdays and Sundays; 212-243-5343. This
was a favorite haunt of Andy Warhol. About 200
dealers.
• *Kutztown and Adamstown, PA:* Renninger's
Antique Markets; held weekly; 717-385-0104.
About 250 dealers exhibit Saturday in Kutztown
while twenty miles away, at Adamstown, 600
dealers appear on Sundays.
• *Atlanta, GA:* Scott Antique Market, Atlanta
Exposition Center. Held second weekend of every
month; 614-569-4912. 1,200 dealers.
• *Springfield, OH:* Springfield Antique Show &
Flea Market; held monthly except July; 513-325-
0053. Call for dates of the two annual Extrava-
ganza weekends when more than 2,000 dealers
show.
• *Centerville, MI:* Caravan Antiques Market; held
second Sunday of every month, May through
October; 312-227-4464.
• *St. Charles, IL:* Kane County Flea Market, about
40 miles west of Chicago; held first Sunday and
preceding Saturday of every month; 708-377-2252.
1,500 dealers.
• *Canton, TX:* First Monday Trade Days; held
monthly; 214-567-6556. Nearly 3,000 dealers
gather for four days before the first Monday of
every month.
• *Pasadena, CA:* Rose Bowl Flea Market; held
second Sunday of every month; 213-587-5100. Has
1,500 dealers from all over the West and Midwest.

Antique Shops
These small stores exist in nearly every town and in
all the major cities. Antique shops can offer a wide
variety of merchandise or they may specialize.
Prices at sophisticated metropolitan shops, where

rent is high, are often inflated, although finding fairly priced items is not out of the question. You'll probably do better, however, to start with suburban and country shops. In vacation areas, items will be overpriced during the season—the summer months at the beach, and winter on the ski slopes.

To get the most out of an antique shop, quietly look at all the items of interest. Buy *only* those that are fairly priced or underpriced and that are part of your specialty. Then ask to speak to the shop owner. Tell him or her of your interest and ask if they have other items in storage or if they can suggest other local shops to visit.

It pays to develop an ongoing relationship with an honest antique shop owner. He or she will then call you when something comes in that might add to your collection.

General Auctions

An auction is a special type of sale. Items for sale are held up in front of the room and people in the audience raise their hands to **bid** for them. The items go to the highest bidder. Auctions are regularly held throughout the country. Public announcements of the auction and its contents are made prior to the date of the sale in newspapers and publications devoted to collectibles.

Auctions are often held in order to settle an **estate** or a **bankruptcy,** or because someone who is moving does not want to take his or her possessions to a new setting. Collectibles are also placed for sale in an auction when the owner wants cash or wants to upgrade or improve his or her holdings.

Good auctions draw large crowds and can last anywhere from two to ten hours; some run several days. On pages 30-37 you can learn how to bid for collectibles at an auction.

Bid: The amount offered for an item being sold at an auction.

Estate: All the assets a person owns at the time of his or her death.

Bankruptcy: When individuals or businesses cannot pay their debts and their assets are sold to raise money.

Estate Sales

There are often many items in an estate that have
some value but that the heirs do not want. They
then decide to sell them in an estate sale. Notices of
the sale are placed in a local newspaper, listing the
items to be sold. On the day of the sale, the public
lines up outside the deceased's home or apartment,
waiting for admission. The managers of the sale try
to sell everything in the house within two to three
days by pricing the items reasonably. Buyers know
this, so competition for the best items is keen. It's
best to arrive early if you think there is something
you want for your collection.

Conventions and Shows

These large gatherings, which are advertised in
trade and specialty publications, feature hundreds of
collectibles. Prices often are higher than at other
types of sales because the merchandise is considered by most knowledgeable collectors to be of a
higher quality. Conventions and shows are an
excellent place in which to learn about collectibles,
to meet other collectors, and to talk to reliable,
experienced experts.

Fellow Collectors

As you become active in the field of collecting, you
will gradually meet other collectors with similar
interests. You will meet them at conventions, by
joining a collector's club, or through the mail—
having read their ads in a specialty publication.
Collectors tend to sell items to each other at less
than the retail price because there is no dealer
markup or commission.

Dealers

Dealers are also a valuable source of collectibles
and they provide a number of services. New or

COMMON TERMS USED AT AUCTIONS

•*Buyers' pool*. Sometimes called a "buyers' ring," this is a conspiracy by a group of buyers, often dealers, to hold the bidding down on key items in order to increase their profits. Several dealers who would normally be bidding against each other agree who will buy each item and what the top bid will be. When that item comes up, the others don't bid in an effort to keep the price low. After the auction, the members of the buyers' pool sell the pieces to one another.

•*Call-ups*. When the crowd is unenthusiastic or beginning to dwindle, an auctioneer may ask the audience if there are any "call-ups," that is, if they would like to request that a certain item be held up for sale as soon as possible, out of the order presented in the catalog. If there are, those items would be bid on next.

•*Choice*. This means the final bidder has his or her choice of the final items up for sale. Usually you have the option of taking any number of them, from one to all. For example, if four chairs were sold "choice," you could take any one of them for $50 or any combination for $50 each.

•*Consignments*. To strengthen what might not be a big sale, auctioneers may take pieces on consignment and sell them along with other items. Consignments generally come from individuals selling part of their collection, from antique dealers or from the auctioneer himself who has items left over from a previous sale.

•*Estate sale*. This term indicates that the items for sale are from a private collection and not from a dealer's stock, and therefore are new to the market.

•*Jumping the bid*. The auctioneer will take bids in incremental amounts called jumps. For example, if he takes $5 jumps, then the bidding will go from $10 to $15 to $20 and so on. Jumping bids is a ploy used by bidders to get rid of other interested bidders by jumping the bid. Let's say an antique toy train that has been progressing steadily in price at $5 jumps is now up to $150. You've decided you will go as high as $225. Rather than let the momentum build, you "jump the bid" to $200.

•*Minimum or reserve.* The auctioneer may allow the owner of a consigned collectible to set a minimum bid that the piece must reach to be sold. It is designed to protect consignors.

•*Salting the auction.* When an auction is advertised as an estate sale (see above) but the auctioneer has added items for sale from others, including his own stock, this is known as salting the auction. Reputable auctioneers will indicate this when this is the case, identifying the source of each item.

•*Shill.* A person planted in the audience by an auctioneer to keep the bidding going on items that are not selling well or for less than their full value. This, of course, is an unethical practice.

•*So much apiece, take all.* Used with sets, such as glasses, chairs, etc., where you bid on just one of them but your final purchase price will be the last bid times the number of pieces. For example, if a set of four chairs is up for bid, the auctioneer announces that they will be sold "so much apiece, winner take all." If the final bid is $50, then the bidder will pay $50 times four, or $200.

•*Unrestricted.* This word on sale or auction notices means the auctioneer or seller has not set a minimum price on the items.

Calling for bids at an auction

smaller dealers often work out of their homes; the major dealers have their own shops and control the bulk of investment-grade and highly desirable collectibles that are sold to the public. They have access to a large amount of cash as well as to leading collections and are extremely important to the serious collector. A reliable dealer will indicate the authenticity of the object being sold. Many dealers allow good customers to take home a piece for several days to see if they like it. Dealers often establish close working relationships with collectors when they locate them. The top dealers advertise in the leading trade publications, such as *Antiques Magazine, Connoisseur, Apollo,* and *Hobbies.*

Pawnshops

Despite their image as skid-row storefronts operated by loan sharks, pawnshops are often legitimate businesses that offer bargains. They carry everything from computers to antiques. Many accept credit cards.

When a person goes to a pawnbroker for money, personal property, such as a watch, is used for **collateral.** The pawnbroker lends the individual a fraction of the watch's value and, after an agreed-upon period, the debtor repays the loan with interest to redeem the watch. Interest rates are set by state statute, so they vary from one state to another.

Collateral: An asset pledged to a lender until a loan is repaid.

About 80 percent of debtors redeem their possessions. But when people fail to redeem an object, the pawnbroker forecloses and puts the item up for sale. Thus, a pawnbroker can offer excellent prices on merchandise because he is trying to recover only the loan—an amount that represents a portion of the collateral's value.

Before doing business with a pawnshop, ask your local Better Business Bureau or Chamber of

Commerce about the shop's reputation and find out
if there have been any complaints filed against it.

Yard Sales and Garage Sales

An estimated six million to nine million yard sales
are held each year in this country, with some $1
billion changing hands. Pricing at these sales is,
more often than not, pure guesswork. To be successful, get to know the going rate for common
items by visiting several yard sales in your area.
And try to arrive early to beat out other collectors.
Serious shoppers arrive early. Most of these sales
require cash, although some sellers accept traveler's
and personal checks with adequate identification.

For More Information

• Magazines:

   The Antique Trader Weekly has a national
calendar of flea markets. For a free copy, write to:

   P.O. Box 1050
   Dubuque, IA 52001
   319-588-2073

• Books:

   Flea Market Price Guide by Robert W. Miller.
Radnor, PA: Wallace-Homestead Book Co., 1984;
5th edition.

   Flea Market Trader by Bob and Sharon
Huxford. Paducah, KY: Collector Books, 1989; 6th
edition.

   *The Official Directory to the United States Flea
Markets.* New York: House of Collectibles, 1988;
2nd edition.

Auctions: How Not to Get Hammered

Many collectibles can be found at shops, galleries, shows, and through dealers. When you buy from these sources, you have plenty of time to study the object and make up your mind. Yet wonderful items can also be found at auctions. Here the gavel swings fast and decisions must be made quickly. There's no time for hesitation. Despite this pressurized atmosphere, collectors cannot afford to shy away from auctions. You might find just what you've been looking for.

Auctions have been a way to exchange goods as far back as the second century A.D. when the Romans used them for selling war booty. In the 17th century in Holland, perishable foods were sold at auctions. Art auctions soon followed and by the middle of the 18th century there were some sixty auctioneers in London alone. Two of them are still in business today: Sotheby's and Christie's.

Learning the Ropes

There's nothing quite like the excitement and drama of an auction.

Yet an auction is like a three-way tug-of-war—a tussle between the owner of the item up for sale, the auctioneer, and the buyers. These bidding duels are not for the naive. If you follow these guidelines, you'll minimize mistakes and come away with the right item at just about the right price.

• *Before the auction.*

1) *Do your homework.* Study up on the item for which you will be bidding. Know the price range for this type of piece.

2) *Look before you leap.* Before bidding, attend several auctions. Become familiar with the feeling and procedures.

TOOLS OF THE TRADE

Always arm yourself with the proper tools of the trade when going to an auction—or when looking for collectibles anywhere. The following tools will help you determine quality and authenticity as well as alert the seller to the fact that you're a serious collector, not an amateur. Keep them together in a tote bag or knapsack.

•The auction catalog. Record the sale prices for future reference in the catalog.

•Pen and pad of paper. Make notes about prices, condition of items, who bid, sale price (if no catalog), and names and telephone numbers of dealers and other people you meet and may want to call upon in the future.

•Small flashlight with a set of fresh batteries. Use to thoroughly examine the collectible under consideration. Look in corners and crevices. Take out drawers. Turn the piece upside-down and inside-out. Check for identification marks, signs of repair, chips, cracks, and other flaws. Auction display rooms, dealer's shops, and old barns are often poorly lit and flaws may be hard to see.

•Magnifying glass. Use at least a 6-power one, and preferably 10-power, to examine collectibles for dates, signatures and autographs, cracks, repairs, breaks, and other small details.

•Tape measure. Large objects, furniture, and paintings should always be measured. Otherwise they may not go through your front door.

•Battery-operated ultraviolet lamp. To detect flaws and repairs not seen by the naked eye.

•Loupe. This special jeweler's magnifying glass reveals scratches and other marks on gems and pieces of jewelry.

•Small magnet. This enables you to tell the difference between a brass-plated, brass painted, or solid brass item.

•A general price guide. Keep a paperback edition of *Kovel's Antiques & Collectibles Price List* or another standard guide with you as a reference book.

3) *Read the catalog.* If there is a catalog for the auction, purchase it in advance. It will give dollar estimates as well as a description of the items for sale. During the auction, write down what each item sold for and use the catalog as a price guideline in the future.

4) *Attend the preview before the sale.* Study the **lots** on display and make notes in your catalog of their size, age, condition, etc. Take the tools of the trade with you: a pen and pad of paper, a small flashlight, a magnifying glass, and a tape measure. At the preview be a real snoop: open drawers, look for cracks, plug in lamps, turn over items, look for identifying marks, etc. Ask the staff questions. Scrutinize each item of interest. Always measure large pieces.

Lots: An item or a group of items sold together at an auction.

5) *Make a written list of the items you really want.* Don't give in to "auction fever" and buy everything in sight.

6) *Set a dollar limit before the auction.* Write it down and stick to it.

7) *Bid absentee.* If you are not able to go to the auction, ask if you can submit a bid, by mail or telephone, giving the top dollar amount you are willing to pay. The auction house will provide precise and detailed instructions. Most catalogs have a form for mail bids, sometimes called a "bid sheet." You must establish credit in advance to place such a bid.

And remember, everything at an auction is "as is"—there's no taking it back next week because you didn't notice a scratch or that the item was crooked.

• *At the auction.*
Here are the steps to follow when attending an auction.

Before an auction it is advisable to check out items for value and condition.

Step 1. After registering, you will be given a number and something to bid with, most likely a paddle.

Step 2. Find out what the incremental dollar amounts are. Some auctioneers move up by $10; others by $100. Ask or check the catalog.

Step 3. If you don't want your bidding noticed, sit either near the front, a little to the side so you can see other people bidding, or in the back rows.

Step 4. Listen to the bidding terminology carefully. "Silver looking" is not the same as "sterling silver." Never place a bid until you are at

ease with the auctioneer's voice and patter. Know
if you are bidding by the piece or by the lot.

Step 5. Pay attention to the orchestration of the
auction. The most important items for sale are
usually brought out toward the middle, when the
crowd is fullest and it has been "warmed up." After
the major items have been sold, the crowd may be
thinned out, leaving less competition for the remaining items. This is a good time to bid, provided the
items you're interested in have not been sold.

Step 6. Don't be the first to bid on an item you
want. Auctioneers often set an arbitrary opening
price which may turn out to be artificially high, in
which case it will drop if there are no bidders.
Watch who else is bidding. You don't want to be
bidding against yourself. Then bid as you sense the
price rising or that it's near the top.

SOLD! The last and winning bid is the hammer
price. This is what you pay plus, in many cases, a
percentage fee to the auction house. This extra
percentage is called a buyer's premium. If you are
the winner, make a note of your bidding number
and the lot number. When you pick up your items,
bring these numbers along. Auctioneers try to keep
their records straight, but slip-ups do occur.

Legally, you are obliged to take what you
successfully bid for at an auction. If you have
second thoughts or change your mind, some auction
houses will let you return an item—provided you
shoulder the cost of resale. However, this is the
exception rather than the rule. You should plan on
putting your money where your bid was. And don't
forget to plan for transporting what you purchased
home. It's a good idea to take along several boxes
and some rope, especially if you're planning to bid
on small items, such as dishes or old toys. Larger
houses can arrange for delivery, but if you're at a

country auction, you'll need a car or a station wagon. If you're collecting pinball machines or old juke boxes, a pickup truck is necessary.

Reading Auction Catalogs

Auction catalogs are excellent resources and deserve careful reading. Sometimes they are available several weeks in advance of the sale, giving you time to do some comparison shopping and to study the subject area. Here are the major points you will find in catalogs:

1) *Terms of the sale*

• Bidding requirements. You may have to get a numbered paddle.

• Deposit requirements. Returnable the same day if you don't buy.

• Method of payment. Cash, traveler's checks, certified checks, credit cards.

• Absentee bids. Directions for how to place an absentee bid by mail or phone. (You must specify your top bid. A staff person or the auctioneer will then bid for you at the actual auction.)

• Pickup. When you can claim your purchases.

• Fees. So-called buyer's fees or premiums that are added on to the purchase price.

2) *Policy on reserves*

Although all items are for sale to the highest bidder, in practice it doesn't always work quite that way. Some lots have a "reserve," or minimum price. If a lot does not bring this price it can be withdrawn. Some auction houses use an "R" or some other symbol to designate that a lot has a reserve price.

3) *Descriptive statements*

These are often given for noted artists, craftsmen, and designers. Note carefully such phrases as "attributed to the artist," and "in the school of."

These indicate that the experts are not certain the work is indeed by a certain person.

4) *Descriptive information*

This material tells about the style, patterns, colors, ounces, measurements. The term "style" often signals a reproduction. For example, a Queen Anne chair means the piece is from the period when Queen Anne ruled England, but a Queen Anne style chair means it is a reproduction of that style.

5) *Guarantees or warranties*

Catalogs do make mistakes. If you buy something described as mahogany and it turns out to be walnut, or if an item is described as silver and it's really silver plate, you may have a claim against the auction house.

6) *Presale estimates*

Estimates represent the auctioneer's opinion based on the current market. If you're interested in an item and it seems way above your price, don't give up. The estimate may be too high, interested people may not show up—any number of things can happen that reduce the actual sale price. (*Note:* If you don't want to buy a catalog, presale estimates are generally posted at the auction house.)

For More Information

• Contact these houses for copies of their catalogs as well as news of forthcoming auctions:

Bowers and Merena Galleries, Inc.
P.O. Box 1224
Wolfeboro, NH 03894

Butterfield & Butterfield
220 San Bruno Avenue
San Francisco, CA 94103

Christie's
502 Park Avenue
New York, NY 10022

Du Mouchelle's
409 East Jefferson Avenue
Detroit, MI 48226

Garth's Auctions, Inc.
2690 Stratford Road
Delaware, OH 43015

Hake's Americana
Box 1444
York, PA 17405

Phillips
406 East 79th Street
New York, NY 10021

C.G. Sloan & Co.
4920 Wyaconda Road
Rockville, MD 20852

Sotheby's
1334 York Avenue
New York, NY 10021

• For more information on forthcoming auctions, consult these trade papers at your library, or subscribe:

The Antiques and Arts Weekly
Bee Publishing Company
Newtown, CT 06470
(203) 426-3141

The Antique Trader Weekly
P.O. Box 1050
Dubuque, IA 52001
(319) 588-2073

The Maine Antique Digest
P.O. Box 358
Waldoboro, ME 04572
(207) 832-7534

Hunting for Value and Quality

Whether you're looking for your first or fiftieth
purchase, you should always aim for value and
quality. The value of a collectible is a continually
changing factor. It depends on how many people
want it, whether the style is popular, where it is
being sold (certain auction houses, for instance,
command higher prices than others), and what
similar objects are being sold at the same time.
Rarity, age, and condition also determine value.

In general, something brand new, whether it is
individually hand-crafted or mass-produced, almost
always goes down in price immediately after its
appearance on the market. In fact, the price seems
to automatically drop for the first 20 to 25 years.
The experts call this a "period of obsolescence." If,
after that time period, the piece is in good condition
and is unique or rare, it often emerges from obscu-
rity and suddenly becomes a hot collectible. When
an object becomes approximately 100 years old, it
is recognized as an antique.

Another important factor in determining value is
condition. The better an item's condition, the
greater its potential value. An item in perfect
condition (no cracks, wrinkles, smudges, tears,
repairs) will command the best price and is almost

always worth more than the same item with flaws.

Rarity is also important. A rare item in top condition is highly prized. Therefore, save your money to buy one really great piece rather than several flawed ones. Or, if you already own several flawed pieces, trade up in order to improve your collection.

Value is also affected by authenticity. Reproductions, no matter how fine they are, are never as valuable as the real thing. Therefore, the artist's signature or initials and a date, if genuine, add to the value of any collectible.

Unexpected events also can affect value. For example, the value of a certain type of collectible can explode when someone writes the first major article or book on the topic or when a museum holds an exhibition for a long-ignored area. And value can collapse just as fast if an artist, style, or category falls from favor with the public.

To develop an eye for value and quality, visit museums, reputable dealers, and auction houses. Study the best examples. You'll soon be able to discern between real and fake, between high quality and tacky junk.

GRETA GARBO'S COLLECTION

This famous film star, who died April 15, 1990, at the age of 84, left her entire estate to her niece and her niece's four children. Included were about 250 items she kept in her seven-room Manhattan apartment overlooking the East River. Among Garbo's collectibles were three Renoir paintings, which she purchased in the 1940s; many pieces of 18th-century French furniture; decorative rugs; rare books; and Continental, English, and Chinese ceramics. The Swedish-born actress, known for being reclusive, starred in 27 movies, including "Anna Christie," "Anna Karenina," "Camille," and "Mata Hari."

Greta Garbo

Stores that specialize in baseball memorabilia are popular with collectors.

3

THE BUYING PROCESS

O f course, in the process of putting together a collection of items you love, decision-making can become emotional. Buying based on emotion does not always result in the best value—you're apt to pay too much because you love something. It is important to learn to balance the emotional and the sensible when assembling a collection. Although collecting is first and foremost for fun, you can also aim to collect for profit. It is exciting to own something that has true value or whose value grows over time.

The Secrets of Successful Buying

Don't expect to make an instant fortune, though. You may have heard about collectibles that made their owners lots of money—a 1935 Mickey Mouse lunch box that sold for $35,000 or a rare American gold coin that brought the seller thousands of dollars—but these are exceptions, not the rule.

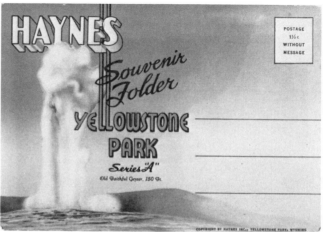

Count on having a good time, not making a fortune, when assembling your collection.

How to Make Great Buys

These basic guidelines will help you assemble a valuable collection, whether it is comic books, Coke bottles, or toy soldiers.

1) *Buy only what you like.* If, later on, the value should drop or you decide to sell part of your collection and keep this particular item, you will own something you love. Ask yourself: "Do I like it?" Or, "Will I use it?"

(Opposite page, top)
A needle case

(Bottom)
A postcard

(This page, left)
Cover of a recipe book

(Above)
A soap ad

2) *Buy the best you can afford.* The better the condition of a collectible, the greater its value. Condition is not an emotional decision. It is a factual one.

3) *Set a dollar amount.* This can be revised each year. Never take all your allowance or savings and invest it in an exotic collectible. If you should need money when you go to college or leave home and all your cash is tied up in baseball cards, you will be forced to sell your collection. If prices are low when you sell, you may not break even.

4) *Put together a collection.* A collection is worth more than the total of its individual parts.

Collections increase in value over time more than a single object.

5) *Specialize.* Random collecting tends to be less valuable over the years than a specialized collection. After selecting an overall collectible category, specialize, focusing on an individual artist, period, craftsman, or country. Unrelated pieces have less marketability than a cohesive, well thought-out collection.

6) *Question seeming bargains.* Don't hope to get something for nothing or very little. If an item is priced so low that it appears to be a bargain, look carefully. Examine the seller's motive. True, undiscovered gems do exist at sales, but for the most part, dealers, auction houses, and regulars at flea markets know their merchandise. In fact, they probably know it better than you do.

7) *Buy in your price range.* If your budget is limited, begin small. As circumstances and your finances improve, so can your collection.

8) *Buy when you see it.* Don't let an item of good value get away because it doesn't seem like a great bargain. If it interests you, fits in with your specialty, and is not overpriced, buy it. It probably won't be there the next time you're in the shop or at a flea market.

A Word of Caution

Don't be misled by ads for "limited editions" or "collector's items" that appear in many magazines. They are often of collector's plates, ceramic figurines, birds and animal figures, and silver items. The ads indicate that the exclusive editions will increase so much each year. The fact is these so-called "limited" editions are often factory-made and produced in the tens of thousands. Things that are produced in such high quantities are unlikely to have lasting monetary value.

Before You Buy

You can cut down the chances of making a poor purchase if you:

1) Study the field or fields you're most interested in.

2) Always carry a high-quality magnifying glass—you never know when you may come across a find.

3) Examine all objects in good light; many antique shops are dimly lit for a reason. Insist on taking the items outdoors for a good look.

4) Know the item's condition.

ANDY WARHOL'S COLLECTION: THE GARAGE SALE OF THE CENTURY

A silver and rosewood tea set. A Superman touch-tone phone. World War II medals. Eighteen-karat gold nail scissors. A wooden merry-go-round horse. The ten-day auction of Andy Warhol's collectibles, held in the spring of 1988 at Sotheby's in New York, was one of the most extensive estate sales in history. It attracted more than 45,000 collectors and curiousity seekers, including the King and Queen of Sweden, Bianca Jagger and Dick Cavett. The writer, Fran Lebowitz, who wandered around the nearly two-acre display of memorabilia in Sotheby's auction rooms, said it was "like being in a theme park."

Warhol, the pop artist who turned the Campbell soup can and Brillo pad into an art form, died in 1987. Until then, the extent of his collection was largely a secret known only to close friends and dealers. Yet his huge town house on the Upper East Side of Manhattan was so cluttered with the results of his buying binges that only two or three rooms were inhabitable. Warhol even stuffed Picassos in closets! David Bourdon wrote in the auction catalog: "He was chronically, almost neurotically acquisitive…forever searching for that mythical five dollar find that would turn out to be worth at least $1 million."

The most frenzied bidding at the auction was for Warhol's 152 cookie jars from the 1930s and 1940s. A lot whose value Sotheby's had estimated at $100 to $150 went for $23,100. One businessman purchased 136 of the cookie jars for a total of $198,605. A Miss Piggy and Kermit the Frog beach towel and other Muppet memorabilia went for $1,760. A Fred Flintstone quartz watch, with the original Bloomingdale's price tag of $20 on it, sold for $2,640.

Andy Warhol

Valuable bottles may be found among throwaway items.

4

PROTECTING YOURSELF

I mitation is said to be the highest form of flattery. That may be so with friendships and style, but watch out for imitations when you are collecting. Imitations, reproductions and look-alikes never have the same value as an original.

Fakes, however, are a fact of life in the world of collectibles. Even great museum directors and curators have been fooled.

Detecting Fakes

There are several ways you can protect yourself from fakes. Your main defense is knowing as much as you can about a given field. Know what materials were used, how the item was put together, who the designers or manufacturers were, what colors and motifs they used, what finishes were favored, and how they were applied. This information is available in specialized books, from courses on collectibles, by talking with knowledgeable collectors and dealers, and finally, from experience.

A more immediate way to protect against fakes and forgeries is to obtain written proof of an item's authenticity.

Although most dealers and sellers are honest, you should always be careful. If you are spending sizeable amounts of money, get an independent **appraisal.** (See page 51.) To do this you may have to take the item to the appraiser. If you have established a relationship with a dealer, he or she may let you keep the piece for a limited time to do this. You will, of course, have to leave a deposit, or perhaps the full price. (Always get a receipt).

Appraisal: A written statement stating how much an item is worth in dollars.

In addition to ascertaining authenticity, you must also insist on a detailed bill of sale. This does not mean one that reads: "One tin Coca-Cola tray, $175." A detailed bill of sale helps you with your legal rights if there is a dispute about the object. It should include:

- style
- date of manufacture
- dimensions
- **provenance** (see page 52)
- period
- designer/artist name
- material
- sales history

Provenance: The ownership history of an object. It tells who owned it and when.

Other ways you can avoid being taken:

1) Always remember the first rule of collecting: *caveat emptor,* or "let the buyer beware." That means that you should be careful when buying any item.

2) Always get an appraisal if in doubt about an item's authenticity.

3) Personally examine everything you buy.

4) Be suspicious about items that are way underpriced.

5) Remember that certain phrases such as "school of Van Gogh" or "Queen Anne style" describe something that is *not* the real thing.

6) Get a detailed bill of sale in writing.

7) Obscure country antique shops and auctions are unlikely to be selling famous masters.

8) Buy only from reputable dealers.

Security and Insurance

Once your collection is worth a substantial amount of money, talk to your parents about insuring it. If they have a homeowner's policy, it should be reviewed to see if it covers antiques, artwork, jewelry, and other collectibles. In many cases, these items are not adequately covered and must be specifically added on in what is called a rider. For a superb collection, you may need a "fine arts" policy. To determine how much insurance coverage you should have, arrange for an appraisal.

If your collection is damaged or lost, calling an appraiser after the fact is seldom useful. Instead, photograph or videotape your items and place these pictures along with sales slips in a safe place other than where the collection is kept. Both are proof that you indeed did own twenty Barbie dolls or seven hand-blown perfume bottles from the 1890s.

Inflation or a changing market will influence the value of your possessions and how much the insurance company will pay. For example, if you bought two autographs five years ago for $75 and they are now worth $200, the insurance company will probably only pay $75 if the autographs are lost or stolen. To protect yourself, have your collection appraised regularly—ideally every three years when the collectibles market is moving up.

Other ways to protect your collectibles:

1) Do not display them in a window.

2) Install an alarm system (this may reduce your parents' insurance premium).

3) If your house is on a house tour, put your collection away.

4) If you lend your collection to a school, gallery, museum, or store, do so anonymously. Ask the sponsor to leave your name off the list of exhibitors or donors.

Risks to Be Aware Of

Although a well-informed collector with an understanding of his or her field can deal profitably in collectibles, there are distinct risks one should be aware of.

• *Misrepresentation of Quality*

Collectors must be certain that they are actually getting the merchandise as it is represented. One of the great risks the non-expert faces is winding up with something of lower quality than he thought he had purchased.

• *Volatility of Popular Taste*

All collectibles do not rise in price. Some are short-term fads and decline quickly in value.

• *Reproductions and Forgeries*

Unscrupulous people do attempt to make forgeries of collectibles. To prevent being taken in by this type of person, always get an expert's opinion as to the authenticity of what you're buying. Reproductions should be so labeled.

• *Warehouse Discoveries*

Sometimes a large number of a given collectible is found in a warehouse or in someone's personal files. When these come onto the market, they can drive the price down for all items in the same category.

• *Fragility*

Many collectibles are fragile and do not withstand the rigors of aging. This is particularly true for paper items, glass that can be chipped easily, pottery and porcelain pieces that are easily broken, and metal that will rust if not taken care of.

Getting an Appraisal

What are your collectibles worth? It's not always an easy question to answer. To get an official evaluation or appraisal of your collectible, you will need to hire an appraiser. An appraisal, a statement of an accurate, realistic value of a possession made by a knowledgeable person, is used for establishing an item's worth either for insurance coverage or to determine what price to ask when selling. Appraisals are also required by the Internal Revenue Service when something of value is donated to a charity and the donor wishes to declare a **deduction.** Some appraisals are made to satisfy one's curiosity.

An official appraisal must be written, dated, and signed. It should also indicate whether the appraisal price is the fair market value (used for selling the item, dividing an estate, or donating it to charity) or replacement value (for insurance reimbursement). The object appraised should be described in as much detail as possible and the number of pieces being appraised should be made clear. For example, if the value given is for a pair of candlesticks, a set of 12 buttons, or a 200-piece jigsaw puzzle, these numbers should be noted.

Before hiring an appraiser, ask what he charges for his services. Some appraisers quote a flat fee in advance; others charge an hourly rate. If the appraiser charges by the hour, ask him to estimate how long the job will take. Never use an appraiser who asks to be paid a percentage of the dollar value

Deduction: An expense allowed by the IRS . This expense can be subtracted, or deducted from one's gross adjusted income when figuring out how much federal tax one owes.

of the appraisal. This method encourages the appraiser to over-appraise an item in order to charge the owner more.

Although there are no licensing or educational requirements for becoming an appraiser, you can find a reliable one through the International Society of Appraisers. This group grants associate membership to appraisers who have five years of experience and full membership to those who have completed a training course given by Indiana University at various continuing education sites across the country. Recommendations from a bank's **trust department,** a lawyer, or a museum or gallery are also helpful.

Trust department: A division of a bank that oversees someone's estate.

When interviewing an appraiser, ask if he or she is qualified to make your particular appraisal. If your collection falls outside his area of expertise, he should be willing to call an expert. Inquire about his training and professional experience and ask for references. Verify his information.

The Written Appraisal

A formal appraisal should include these key points:

• A detailed description of the item, including age, size, markings, artist's name, historical association, and rarity.

• The object's *provenance*—its history, who owned it before, and proof of authenticity.

• Statement of original cost and date of purchase.

• A good color photograph of the object.

• A statement of comparables upon which the appraisal was based. This could include sales of other similar objects and prices quoted in dealers' catalogs.

• The date of the appraisal.

• The appraiser's signature.

For More Information

• Courses in appraising antiques and collectibles are
given by:
Indiana University
Independent Study Program
School of Continuing Studies
Owen Hall
Bloomington, IN 47405
812-335-5323 or 800-457-4434

• To locate a reliable appraiser, contact:
American Society of Appraisers
P.O. Box 17265
Washington, DC 20041
703-478-2228

Appraisers Association of America
60 East 42nd Street
New York, NY 10165
212-867-9775

American Gem Society
5901 West Third Street
Los Angeles, CA 90036
213-936-4367

FRANKLIN D. ROOSEVELT'S COLLECTION

While still in grade school, Franklin D. Roosevelt, later to become the thirty-second President of the United Staes, began collecting stamps, birds, and anything related to the sea. When he was ten he took over his mother's stamp collection and added to it each year. By the time he was an adult, the collec-

**President
Roosevelt**

tion had become world famous. When Franklin was eleven, his father taught him how to use a rifle. He soon used it to collect one of every kind of bird in Hyde Park, New York, where he lived. Within a few years, he had a nearly complete collection of stuffed birds from the area displayed in a huge glass case.

A comic book collection can grow in value, as issues become older and more scarce.

HOW TO SELL YOUR COLLECTIBLES

5

fter you've been collecting for a while, you may discover that your Barbie dolls, baseball cards or model trains have taken over your room, filled up the attic, and are overflowing into the garage. If so, it may be time to sell some of them. Of course, there are other reasons why collectors sell: for instance, as you learn more about the items that capture your fancy, you may become dissatisfied with the pieces you initially collected and more interested in upgrading the collection with higher quality items. Or, you may have too many duplicates. And then, of course, you may want to raise cash, perhaps to help pay for college, a car, or something else.

You can easily sell one or two items to an interested friend or collector. Or, you may decide to take advantage of the entrepreneurial opportunity available and set up a small, part-time business, buying and selling collectibles. In fact, most professional dealers started out just like you—as amateur collectors. In this chapter you will learn the basics of the business. For more small business ideas, consult another book in this series, *Entrepreneurship.*

Setting Up a Business

The quickest way to learn the business is to become an **apprentice,** working after school or weekends in the shop of an established antique dealer. Or, you could be a weekend assistant at shows or conventions. Both will give you exposure to well-informed people and to a variety of collectibles. Look in the yellow pages of your phone book for names and ask your parents and friends if they can introduce you to a potential employer.

Apprentice: A person who works for another in order to learn a trade or business.

After gaining some experience, you will be ready to set up your own business. If you run it from home, your **overhead** will be low and most of your money can go into buying and advertising.

Overhead: General costs of running a business other than materials and production; includes rent, and telephone.

There are several preliminary steps to take before opening your doors to customers.

Step 1. *Obtain a sales tax license.* These are issued by states that collect sales tax to retail proprietors. The license both authorizes and requires a dealer to collect state sales tax when he or she sells an item. The tax is a percentage of the total sale price. Each state determines its own percentage. Call your local town hall for information on obtaining an application. You may be referred to the state Treasurer's Office. There is a nominal fee.

Step 2. *Select a name for your business.* It can be as simple as your name: Henrietta Hogarth, Antiques, Inc. or Michael Musselman, Second Hand Treasures. Avoid being too cutesy or picking a name that doesn't get the message across: Simply Wonderful or The Country Chipmunk do not tell potential customers whether you are selling pastries, chipmunks, or used cars.

Step 3. *Have business cards printed.* (See samples.) This will let people know you are serious and where you can be found. When you meet other dealers or potential customers, always give them your card. You can also leave cards at shows and on neighborhood or school bulletin boards.

Step 4. *Set up a bookkeeping system.* This does not have to be a complicated procedure but it must be accurate. It involves two steps: an inventory ledger and an expense journal. These are notebooks with columns drawn in them, available at stationery stores. In the inventory ledger, record purchases, sales and sales tax collected. In the expense journal, keep track of any business expenses you incur, such as advertising costs, equipment, postage, etc. (See sample on page 66.) Keep all receipts for the year in a large envelope with your two books.

Step 5. *Set up a card file.* Record each item you already own and those you purchase along with a description including: size, color, marks, condition, repairs, price paid, to whom, the date purchased and any known history. Ideally each item should be photographed (you can use a Polaroid) and the picture filed behind the card. This card file will also serve as proof of purchase in case any collectibles are stolen, damaged, or lost in a fire or flood. And refer to it for setting sale prices.

Pricing Your Wares

• *Setting a Price.* The biggest dilemma facing everyone selling collectibles is setting a price. There is no one set price for each item. Hot items sell faster and at higher prices than those collectibles currently out of favor. However, there is one constant: quality always sells best.

You certainly want to sell an item for more than you paid for it—but how much more is always a tough question to answer. In this chapter we will give you general guidelines, but ultimately the decision is yours. You will learn by trial and error. Begin by consulting your card file or inventory book. What was the purchase price? Have you spent money on repairs or restoration? Incidentally, repairs and restorations may add or detract from the price. For example, a new coat of paint on an old toy will lower the price. But a table or chair whose loose leg has been tightened is worth more than when it was wobbly. Remember, the original box, label, directions, or other descriptive material that came with an item adds to its value.

Even after looking at all of these factors, as a beginner you may still be uncertain how much to ask. Here are the tricks the pros use to determine prices. Use as many as possible.

1. Consult a knowledgeable collector in the field.

2. Read the classified ads and various articles in current trade publications. In general, if you sell to a dealer your price will be one-third to one-half of these advertised prices. If you sell through the mail, ask full price.

3. Consult a good price guide. If you are selling toy trains, it will tell you what they have gone for in the recent past.

4. Visit shops, auctions, shows, and flea markets. Talk to exhibitors and other dealers. Jot down current prices in your notebook.

5. Get a formal appraisal. Since this is an expensive process, use it only for key items or large lots. Some auction galleries give free appraisals. If the gallery is out of town, call first and ask if you can send a picture and description of the item. Include size, condition, history, provenance, etc. and enclose a stamped, self-addressed envelope.

6. Check the price of comparable new items. For instance, if you want to sell dishes, linens, or silver pieces quickly, price your older items at one-third to one-half the price of the new. Rare pieces, however, generally sell for more than new ones.

7. Consult a matching service. These services buy old silver, glass, or china and resell them to those trying to complete their sets. Their catalogs provide prices you can use as a guideline. They are paricularly useful for standard items, such as Haviland china, Rogers silverware, or Fostoria crystal.

Note: Once you know the current retail price for a collectible you still have to price your items. The general rule of thumb is that an antiques dealer needs to double the cost of an item in order to run the business and make a profit. If you sell to other dealers or special collectors, expect to give them at least a 20 percent discount for buying more than one item. Lump sum prices are granted for a quantity purchase—say for ten items or more. If you sell at an auction gallery, they will charge a fee ranging from 10 to 25 percent of the price.

SIGMUND FREUD'S COLLECTION

The father of psychoanalysis, Sigmund Freud, called his interest in collectibles "an addiction second in intensity only to [my] nicotine addiction." (Freud smoked cigars incessantly.) The consulting room where Freud saw his patients and his adjoining study were bursting with oriental rugs, books, pillows, sculptures, stone plaques, and hundreds of antiquities. Collecting was a lifelong project of Freud's. He told a friend, "I have made many sacrifices for my collection of Greek, Roman and Egyptian antiquities, and actually have read more archaeology than psychology."

Sigmund Freud

Bargains can often be found at garage and tag sales.

6

WHERE TO SELL YOUR COLLECTIBLES

Once you've determined the value or price of your collectibles, you're ready to take the next step: deciding where to sell them. In this chapter we will look at the key places to sell, whether you have just one or two items or are running a small, part-time business as a dealer. Keep in mind that each of these outlets is also a place to look for collectibles to buy.

Classified Ads

Put an ad in the classified section of a trade publication or your area's newspaper. Most use the heading "Antiques (or Collectibles) For Sale." Antique dealers, auctioneers, collectors, and many other people read this section of the classifieds and those who are serious will pick up the phone and call the seller. Study existing ads carefully before writing

yours. Waste no words but give the pertinent facts.
A successful ad lets the potential buyer know
exactly what is for sale and how they can arrange to
see it. Be factual, not romantic, and avoid words
such as beautiful, fantastic, gorgeous, and exquisite.
For example:

> **ANTIQUE SILVER TEA STRAINER.**
> **Circa 1860. English. In original**
> **box. Family heirloom. $300. Call**
> **624-5124 evenings.**

Tell your family that your are running an ad so if
you are not home when people call, they will take
down all the pertinent information.

You will notice that some sellers do not advertise a price. However, by listing the price you
eliminate bargain hunters and a great many useless
calls. The price initiates positive action and in-
creases the percentage of serious lookers.

When a caller expresses interest, arrange for
him or her to see the item as soon as possible while
their enthusiasm is at its peak. Show the piece in a
quiet, well-lit place away from the rest of the
household activity—perhaps in your room, the
garage, or attic. And don't give the impression
you've been using the piece on a day-to-day basis.
It should be cleaned, polished, shined, pressed, and
in working order. If it's a dresser, a trunk, a table
with drawers or some other type of container, clean
out its contents.

Once you and a buyer have settled on a price,
formalize the sale with a receipt (see example).
Always have your receipt book and a pen close at
hand. Then, while the buyer is writing out a check
or adding up cash, you can write out a description
of the piece on the sales receipt. Indicate the

DATE _Feb. 18, 1990_

NAME _Jane Greene_

ADDRESS _23 Oak Hill Road_

CITY _Marveldale_

SOLD BY	CASH	CHARGE	DEPOSIT	C.O.D.
R. L.		X		

QUAN.	DESCRIPTION	PRICE	AMOUNT
1	Civil War Newspaper - 1864	10.00	10.00
2	Narrow-necked green bottles	7.00	14.00

amount paid and figure out the sales tax. Ask for the buyer's name, address, and phone number. Use a receipt book that has carbonless copies so both you and the buyer have identical receipts.

Small purchases are usually paid for in cash. But since most people do not carry large amounts of cash with them, checks are used for bigger ticket items. Unfortunately, sooner or later you're likely to get a "bounced check"—one returned to you by the bank with "Insufficient Funds" stamped on it. You will learn over time to recognize the type of person who tries to pass a bad check, although even the most seasoned dealer can be fooled. The best rule to follow: If you feel at all uneasy about the person, tell him or her you have a cash-only policy and offer to hold the piece until they return with the cash. Ask for a cash deposit of 10 to 15 percent of the sales price in exchange for a detailed receipt.

START-UP EQUIPMENT FOR A DEALER

- Business cards
- Sales slips
- Ledger and inventory books
- Gift-wrapping paper and ribbon
- Marking pens or crayons
- Mailing paper and twine
- Boxes and shopping bags
- Stationery and postage
- Shop sign
- Paper tags with pins or string

Dealers

If you decide to sell to a dealer, select one who specializes in your area. Don't try to sell baseball cards to someone focusing only on movie posters. To find a specialist, ask other dealers, at art galleries, antique shops, or contact one of the national appraisal societies listed at the end of this chapter. Although going in armed with an appraisal gives a seller a sense of what the item is worth, the dealer will probably offer considerably less. To stay in business, the dealer must double his money, which means his markup may be as much as 100 percent. Therefore, you can expect to get somewhere between 35 percent and 80 percent of the appraised value of your collectible.

Consignment: A method of selling an object that involves turning it over to someone else, usually a shopkeeper.

If you are not pleased with the dealer's offer, see if he will take the item on **consignment.** If he then sells it, you get the selling price minus his commission, which will be about 10 percent to 25 percent.

Consignment Shops

These shops, listed in the yellow pages, take other people's collectibles and charge a commission for selling them. There are also some antique shops that will take merchandise on consignment for sale

along with their own items. Visit the shop first to
see if your items fit in with the overall inventory.
Then, if you strike a deal, get a signed, written copy
of the consignment agreement that includes all
charges, how long your item will be offered, and
how it will be insured while in the shop. You, in
turn, should write a detailed description of the items
you're putting on consignment, indicating if a piece
is in mint condition, worn, has flaked paint, extensive repairs, etc. Then if it doesn't sell and you take
it back, you can verify if it has been damaged in the
store. If the item has not sold within several weeks,
the price may be too high.

Flea Markets, Conventions, and Antique Shows

Offer to sell your items to dealers who have dis-
plays or stands at these markets and shows. If the

INVENTORY RECORD

Henrietta's Antiques

Purchases

Date	Seller/Address, Tel.	Item	Price	Sales Tax
8/12/90	Country Antiques Route #4 Oskaloosa, IA 515-227-0800	Greta Garbo Autograph	$110	8%

Sales

Date	Price	Sales Tax	Buyer/Address, Tel.
10/10/90	$185	8%	Ralph Jones 98 Elm Street Des Moines, IA 515-941-8793

EXPENSE JOURNAL

Date	Supplies	Rent	Tel.	Travel	Advertising	Misc.
6/1/90	$25 (stamps)					
6/11/90						$5
6/27/90					$15 (ad in	(lunch)
6/30/90				$8.12 (paid	"Pennysaver")	
				to parents)		

item is large, take a picture with a description instead. Find a dealer selling the same or similar items and wait until the booth or stand is empty. Then ask if he or she is interested in your collectibles. Most dealers look for reasonably priced, good quality items because buying is hard work. Most will ask you to set the price. Add 20 percent to the lowest price you will accept and negotiate from there. The dealer, of course, will want to sell it for twice that amount.

Another option is to set up your own booth. Although it involves a lot of packing and unpacking, selling at a flea market or show can be fun and profitable. Your local newspaper will list flea markets. Call the sponsor and ask the rental fee—it may be as low as $25 for the day for a table at a flea market, or as much as several thousand dollars at a prestigious show. Before setting up your first booth, visit several shows or help a dealer do a show. Ask to meet the show manager. Most shows and flea markets are organized by a professional manager, although a few are run by committees. These people determine which dealers can participate. Some shows have sponsors. If there is one it is usually a charitable organization, museum, hospital, or church trying to raise funds for their cause. The show takes in money by charging admission to the public, by renting booths or tables, and by selling food.

If you decide to participate, ask what happens in case of rain, if there is a lunch stand, and how early you can set up. Find out how large a space you will have and if there is a wall you can hang things on. In most cases, you will receive a contract that will spell out what the manager will provide.

Auctions

Another alternative is to use an auction house. As a general rule, the seller is charged 10 percent of the hammer price for items above a certain amount and 15 percent for lower cost items. If the item does not sell, expect a charge of 5 percent of the "reserve," the minimum price that the seller and the auction house agreed upon. Each auction house varies, so check these figures carefully.

Higher priced items generally bring the most money when sold on the international market by a major auction house. These items are usually worth $10,000 or more. Regardless of the price of your item, first get an independent appraisal (not from the auction house). Then get a presale estimate— the price the auction house believes your item will bring. This figure will be used in the auction catalog and in advertising. If the auction house suggests a lower estimate just before the auction, you can withdraw the object. (A low estimate will probably bring low bids.) To avoid hidden charges, ask for a list of all fees before the sale.

Mail Order

A number of collectibles are bought and sold through the mail. Of course, certain items, such as large pieces of furniture, simply don't lend themselves to being shipped easily by parcel post.

What to Take to a Flea Market or Show

- Umbrella
- Folding chair
- Money box
- Bags
- Sunglasses
- Staple gun
- Scissors
- Extension cord
- Sweater
- Lunch
- Receipt book
- Wrapping paper
- Hat
- Hammer
- Thumb tacks
- Pliers
- Raincoat
- Thermos
- Pens
- Boxes
- Friend or assistant
- Screwdriver
- Picture wire and hooks
- Nails and screws

Books, prints, toys, thimbles, political campaign material, and most small items can be sold through the mail quite easily.

Buyers and sellers communicate primarily through specialized publications that run classified ads. These make it extremely efficient to reach interested collectors. As you build up your customer list, you can send out a list of items for sale directly to them and to other dealers. This list should give a full description of each item, including size, marks, condition, and defects. Photocopies of pictures will enhance sales.

You may want to add the cost of mailing to your price. Pricing should also take into consideration the cost of packing materials. Always insure all packages.

Garage and House Sales

People selling a house full of goods often call one of the local house sale firms or auctioneers. They are listed in the yellow pages under "Liquidators." These pros handle everything: advertising, pricing, security, permits, staff, refreshments, and collecting money. You pay them a percentage of all items sold.

When you are only selling a handful of items, join a group of friends or neighbors and put your collectibles in a giant garage sale. Among the guidelines to keep in mind when selling at a garage sale:

1. Get to know the going rate for similar items by visiting several garage or tag sales in your area.

2. Charge 10 percent to 20 percent of retail value for clothing and up to one-third to one-half for other items.

3. Most shoppers will buy anything priced under $2.

4. A neat, attractive display enhances the value of the items.

5. People tend to ignore items that are not priced, so label everything with color-coded dots or removable stickers; or, make all items on one table the same price.

6. Serious shoppers arrive early. Begin selling by 8 A.M. or 9 A.M. and end by 3 P.M. Don't bargain or reduce prices during the first hour or so. Never sell an item for less than what seems fair to you.

7. Check local tax laws; some states or municipalities require a permit and insist that you collect sales tax.

FEATURES THAT ENHANCE PRICE

- Original box
- Proof of provenance
- Direction booklet
- A pair is worth more than a single.

- Mint condition
- Maker's label
- Documents related to the piece
- A full set is worth more than singles.

COLD WAR COLLECTIBLES

The destruction of the Berlin Wall in 1989 created an instant collectible. Pieces of the wall were soon on sale at Bloomingdale's and elsewhere in the United States. According to one estimate, 600,000 Americans have paid up to $12 for fist-size pieces of the concrete wall.

And there are other mementos of crumbling communism. Look for East European propaganda posters, newspapers and fliers announcing rallies as

The Wall

well as commemorative statues and lapel pins of discredited political leaders.

Expand your collection into symbols of American social protest. (The Smithsonian Institution in Washington, DC, has more than 60,000 pieces in its collection.) Look for buttons, T-shirts, banners, posters and announcements of protests, marches, hunger strikes, etc. Handmade items are more valuable than mass-produced ones.

For More Information

•Leading auction houses: see list on pages 36- 38.

•To find individual collectors:

Advertise in club newsletters or in one of the specialized publications (see Part Two). The following periodicals are also useful sources of potential buyers:

Antique Trader Weekly
P.O. Box 1050
Dubuque, IA 52001
319-588-2073

Antiques and Arts Weekly
Bee Publishing Company
Newton, CT 06470
203-426-3141

Antiques & Collecting Hobbies (formerly *Hobbies)*
1006 South Michigan Avenue
Chicago, IL 60605
312-939-4767

The Art/Antiques Investment Report
99 Wall Street
New York, NY 10005
212-747-9500

Art & Antiques Magazine
89 Fifth Avenue
New York, NY 10003
212-206-7050

The Connoisseur
1790 Broadway
New York, NY 10019
212-492-1300

The Magazine Antiques
980 Madison Avenue
New York, NY 10021
212-734-9797

The Maine Antique Digest
P.O. Box 358
Waldoboro, ME 04572
207-832-7534

An old Singer sewing machine ad

A DIRECTORY OF COLLECTIBLES

Advertising

The codfish lays ten thousand eggs,
The homely hen lays one.
The codfish never cackles
To tell you what she's done.
And so we scorn the codfish,
While the humble hen we prize,
Which only goes to show you
That it pays to advertise.

Advertisements from the earliest times provide a visual history of commerce in this country. As collectibles, they cover a broad range of objects, including buttons, calendars, jars, tins, trays, promotional cards, and almost anything with an advertiser's logo on it.

Up until the Civil War, much of the country's business was transacted in small cities, towns, and rural areas, where advertising was simply a sign over the door or handbills that were passed out on the street. In the middle of the nineteenth century, however, the advertising industry began to grow. This growth was epitomized by an Englishman, Thomas Barratt of Pears' Soap, who is reputed to have said: "Any fool can make soap but it takes a clever man to sell it." In 1865, Barratt introduced the American public to his popular British soap and to his clever ads, and he soon became a millionaire. American entrepreneurs—including William Colgate, Jay Morton, Dr. Harvey Kellogg, and others—followed in Barratt's footsteps, having seen that advertising was effective.

Growth in advertising corresponded with the development of color printing techniques. By 1876, the production of color trade or promotional cards was widespread. These cards, about the size of playing cards, were given away by merchants to prospective customers.

At the same time, store packaging was revolutionized. In earlier days, tobacco, tea, and coffee were sold in bulk from large tin storage bins supplied to the merchant by the manufacturer. As competition developed and advertising techniques became more sophisticated, manufacturers began to attract customers by decorating these store bins with product names. Next came the idea of packing the goods in individual containers made of tin. These tins, covered with ads, lined the store owner's shelves. Many of the finest ads from the nineteenth century consist of colorful, post card-type scenes printed on sheets of pewter or tin. Tin Coca-Cola trays are one example.

Among the more popular names to look for in advertising collectibles are: Moxie, Hires Root

Beer, Lucky Strike, Cracker Jack, and Prince Albert Tobacco. Prince Albert ads were the subject of a popular joke. A kid would call a grocery store or tobacco shop and ask if the owner had Prince Albert in a tin. If the owner said yes, the caller would say, "Well, let him out." This joke is said to have increased the sale of Prince Albert Tobacco by half.

You can collect ads produced in the 1800s right up to the 1950s or 1960s. If you're willing to think long term, start collecting today's examples of advertising art.

Ideas for Specializing
- Famous brand names
- Tin objects
- Signs
- Advertising cards
- Calendars

For More Information
- Museums to Contact:
  The New York Historical
  Society
  170 Central Park West
  New York, NY 10024
  212-873-3400

  The Shelburne Museum
  Route 7
  Shelburne, VT 05482
  802-985-3344

  The Smithsonian Institution
  Washington, DC 20560
  202-357-2700

- Clubs and Organizations:
  The Ephemera Society
  P.O. Box 37
  Schoharie, NY 12157
  518-295-7878

- Books
  Handbook of Early Advertising Art (2 vols.) by Clarence T. Hornung; Mineola, NY: Dover Publications, 1956, 1988.

  Advertising Art in the Art Deco Style edited by Theodore Menten; Mineola, NY: Dover Publications, 1975, 1989.

Autographs

What's in a name? Money, if it's someone well known. In fact, certain signatures are worth a small fortune. The discharge papers George Washington signed for his soldiers at the end of the Revolutionary War sold for between $1,000 and $1,350 in the early 1970s. Now they're fetching $3,500 and more. During that same 10-year period, a letter signed by Abraham Lincoln increased in value from $3,000 to nearly $8,000. But the autographs that have gone up the most in price since 1970 are those of movie stars, with Greta Garbo leading the list.

Despite these impressive price moves, autographs can still be collected by kids. Inexpensive autographs are readily available throughout the country and prices for many are very affordable, ranging from about $5 for a Red Buttons' signature to several thousand dollars for Greta Garbo's.

Autographs are sold at auctions, by dealers, and by other collectors. You can also get them for free by writing to your favorite celebrities. Write an intelligent letter about a pertinent topic to a famous person. Enclose a self-addressed stamped envelope. If the topic you raised is of interest, you're likely to get back a personally signed letter.

Keep in mind that a signed letter is worth considerably more than just a signature; a handwritten letter is more valuable than a typed one. *Caution:* A growing number of busy celebrities sign their letters with an Autopen, a patented mass-signing pen machine, often used by politicians. A signature that appears extremely even is a tip-off that an Autopen has been used, but it's often hard to tell when an autograph is real and when it isn't. Even the experts are fooled at times.

Store autographs in acid-free folders and never write, staple, or paste anything on them.

Ideas for Specializing
- Movie stars
- Scientists
- Sports figures
- Famous children
- Politicians

For More Information
- Clubs and Organizations:
  The Manuscript Society
  350 North Niagara Street
  Burbank, CA 91505

  Universal Autograph Collectors Club
  P.O.Box 6181
  Washington, D.C. 20044

- Magazines:
  Autograph Collector's Magazine
  P.O.Box 55328
  Stockton, CA 95205
  209-473-0570
  10 issues; $25 per year

- Books:
  Autographs: A Key to Collecting by Mary A. Benjamin. Mineola, NY: Dover Publications, 1986.

Collecting Autographs for Fun and Profit by Robert W. Pelton. Whitehall, VA: Betterway Publications, 1987.

- Dealers:
  To find a reliable dealer, contact the Universal Autograph Collectors Club (listed above) for the name of a member dealer in your area.

  Order catalogs from these nationally recognized dealers:
  Walter R. Benjamin Autographs
  P.O. Box 255
  Hunter, NY 12442
  516-263-4133

  Hake's Americana & Collectibles
  P.O. Box 1444
  York, PA 17405
  717-848-1333

  Abraham Lincoln Book Shop
  357 West Chicago Avenue
  Chicago, IL 60610
  312-944-3085

Baseball Cards

First introduced in the mid-1800s and still marketed
in large numbers today, baseball cards reflect
America's undying enthusiasm for this national
sport. Over one million Americans collect baseball
cards because they love the game, the players, and
the potential profit.

The first cards were placed in cigarette packs
and tobacco containers as a means of advertising.
Called "T" cards, they were produced by various
tobacco companies. Very few exist today, but those
that do command enormous prices. The Honus
Wagner card, issued between 1909 and 1911 by the
American Tobacco Company, is one of the most
famous cards of all time. It is estimated to be worth
$110,000 today.

In the 1920s, American Caramel, National
Caramel, and York Caramel, all candy manufacturers, began manufacturing cards. Then, from 1933
until 1941, the Goudey Gum Company of Boston

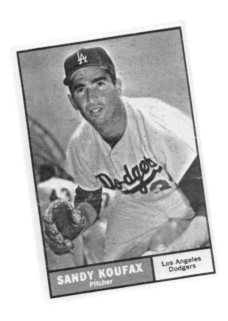

Baseball Card Grading System

The most valuable cards are those that are in prime condition and are scarce issues of popular players. Buyers and sellers use the following scale in determining value.

- *Mint:* A perfect card. Centered with equal borders and four sharp corners. No creases or dents.
- *Near mint:* A nearly perfect card. Flaws show up only under careful scrutiny. A slightly off-center card falls into this category.
- *Excellent:* Card may be off-center, or surface may show loss of luster.
- *Very good:* Signs of handling. Rounded corners or minor creases. Gum, wax, or packaging stains but no major creases or tape marks.
- *Good:* Well-worn card but no serious damage. May have several creases and rounded corners.
- *Fair:* Excessive wear, thumbtack holes, tape, paste, small tears and creases, writing on back, or missing bits of paper.
- *Poor:* Corners or parts torn off. Card may be trimmed or have holes from a paper punch. Pen or pencil marks on the front. General defacement.

and Gum, Inc., were the key producers of cards. It wasn't until 1948 that the successor to Gum, Inc., The Bowman Company of Philadelphia, began the modern era of baseball card manufacturing. Three years later, in 1951, Topps, Inc., of Brooklyn entered the market and in 1965 purchased Bowman. In 1952, Topps issued its first complete set of 409 cards. Topps continues to be the top manufacturer. Four companies, Topps, Fleer, Donruss, and Sportsflics, produce an estimated four to five million cards a year.

You have several choices when it comes to buying this season's cards: single cards, dealer vending cases, the wax pack, or a cello (cellophane) pack. When you buy cards in bulk in boxes con-

HINTS FOR HITTING A HOME RUN

- A player headed for the Hall of Fame should not be sold, unless you need the money. These cards tend to rise in value each year.
- Lifetime superstars hold their value well, generally until retirement. You may want to sell just before that point. Hold if you think they'll make it into the Hall of Fame.
- When uncertain about a player, sell.
- Rookie players are quite volatile and risky. Establish a price goal and take your profits.

taining anywhere from 600 to 800 cards, only 15 to 20 percent of them will have potential value. The rest are called "commons."

- *Dealer vending cases.* These boxes, which contain 500 assorted cards, are packed without bubble gum or other inserts. Originally designed to fit into penny arcade dispensers, they are an excellent way to gather a lot of cards instantly.
- *Wax pack.* Designed for retail sales, the number of cards in a wax pack varies from year to year and from company to company. Many have from fourteen to sixteen cards plus a stick of gum if it's manufactured by Topps, jigsaw puzzle pieces if it's from Donruss, a team logo sticker if it's from Fleer, or a trivia card if its from Score. These wax packs sell for about .50 cents and are covered with an opaque wax paper. There are 36 packs per box.
- *Cello pack.* A cellophane pack has about twice the number of cards as a wax pack and sells for about ten to twenty cents less than the cost of two wax packs. The cellophane wrapper is clear, so you can see the players you're buying on the top and bottom.
- *Rack pack.* Also a retail package, this one contains at least three times as many cards as the wax pack. Six cards are visible from the outside, three on top and three on bottom. Unlike wax and

cello packs, they are virtually impossible to tamper with because of their tight wrapping.

New cards and sets are sold in candy stores and bookshops. Older cards and special collections can be bought from or traded with other collectors or dealers. Auctions, which are advertised in hobby publications and sports collectibles shows, are also good sources. If you live in an area that does not have hobby shops or a collectibles convention, you can buy cards from individual dealers who run ads in magazines and hobby papers, but *caveat emptor*—or buyer beware.

The price of a baseball card set is determined by four factors:

1) *Grade.* The better the condition, the greater the value. A card's value drops immediately if it looks a little shopworn. The rankings for condition are clearly spelled out in the box on page 79. Mint (untouched) cards are hard to find, since most young collectors ripped packages open or tore the cards off the boxes they were on. It's also hard to get full sets of these cards, since some cards appeared only on the backs of less popular cereals that kids refused to eat.

2) *Age.* Older cards tend to be worth more, but not always.

3) *Popularity.* Players that the public adores are always more valuable. If buyers don't want a certain player's card, the fact that it's old becomes almost irrelevant.

4) *Scarcity.* The fewer cards printed, generally the more valuable they are.

5) *Sets.* Complete sets sometimes appreciate faster than a single card of a rising star. That's because sets are harder to assemble. Over the years, Topps sets have appreciated between 5 percent and 10 percent in value annually.

To assemble a valuable card collection, begin by reading the sports pages in your local newspaper. Learn the teams, the players and the sports writers' picks for potentially promising careers. Today's rookie may be next year's star. Then start reading a sports magazine to gain more knowledge. During spring training, a number of annual magazines appear on the newsstands featuring personal and team interviews.

If you buy a set of modern cards and hold onto them, you'll probably have tomorrow's superstars already in your collection as well as those later inducted into the Baseball Hall of Fame. Induction automatically raises the value of a player's card.

When buying cards of the 1980s and 1990s, try never to buy less than mint condition. When you go to sell them, the purchaser will be very fussy. To identify a mint card, start with corners: all four should be sharp and square, not rounded. The borders should all be even, the photo properly centered. If you're buying a large group of cards, check each one for a hidden, off-center specimen.

Other things to avoid: paper bubbles, creases, ink streaks, fuzzy printing, out-of-focus pictures, and gum or wax stains.

Handle your cards as infrequently as possible. Store them in plastic, in special locking cases. If you show your collection at conventions, handle cards carefully during your travels. Torn edges lower their value.

Ideas for Specializing

Because this is a very large field, you need to specialize to build a meaningful collection. For example, you may decide to buy complete sets of a given year or a given manufacturer; or, a card of a particular player for each year he has played. You can also specialize by focusing on players from a certain town, state, or college, or on one team's players. Remember, too, that prices vary by geographic region. Houston Astro cards command a higher price in Houston than they do in Des Moines, Iowa.

Rookie cards are another way to make a grand slam. They are part of the American fascination with having the first of something.

You can also specialize in Kellogg's Cards. From 1970 to 1983, American kids grew up eating cereal and studying baseball cards on the Kellogg's box. Kellogg's sets ranged from 54 to 75 cards each. During this era, base-ball cards were dominated by Topps Gum Company, then the only national, full-scale card issued in the United States.

A key year for Kellogg's cards was 1976, the U.S. Bicentennial year. These cards have a red and blue border surrounding a color photo of the player. There are 57 cards in the Bicentennial set.

In 1983, the final year for Kellogg's, there were 60 cards. Complete sets were available through the mail for $3.95 plus two proof-of-purchase seals. Among the most popular players that year were Rod Carew, Rollie Fingers, Reggie Jackson, and Pete Rose.

Over the years, the best inves-tors have stockpiled complete sets as well as individual players they think will become superstars. To know which ones to buy, you must be informed about the game of baseball and the individual players.

For More Information

• Museums to Contact:
   Burdick Collection
   Metropolitan Museum of Art
   Fifth Avenue at 81st Street
   New York, NY 10028
   212-535-7710

• Clubs and Organizations:
   Society for American Baseball
   Research
   P.O. Box 93183
   Cleveland, OH 44101
   215-575-0500

   Society for American Baseball
   Research
   P.O. Box 323
   Cooperstown, NY 13326

• Magazines:
   Baseball Card Price Guide
   Krause Publications, Inc.
   700 East State Street
   Iola, WI 54990
   715-445-2214
   Monthly; $17.95 per year
   Contact Krause Publications for
   a list of related publications.

   Baseball Hobby News
   4540 Kearny Villa Road
   San Diego, CA 92123
   619-565-2848

Monthly; $18 per year

Beckett Baseball Card Monthly
Beckett Publications
4887 Alpha Road (Suite 200)
Dallas, TX 75244
214-991-6657
Monthly; $19.95 per year
Contact Beckett Publications for
a list of related publications.

• Books:
  *The Complete Book of Baseball
  Cards;* Lincolnwood, IL:
  Publications International, 1989.

*The Sport Americana Baseball
Card Price Guide* by James
Beckett, Edgewater Book Co.,
Box 40238, Cleveland, OH
44140; annual.

*A Beginner's Guide to Baseball
Card Collecting: A Step-by-Step
Guide for the Young Collector*
by Casey Childress and Linda
McKenzie; C. Mack Publica-
tions, 1988.

*How to Buy, Trade, and Invest
in Baseball Cards and Collectibles* by Bruce Chadwick
and Danny Peary; Simon &
Schuster, Inc.

Books

Every Sunday, *The New York Times* and other
major newspapers print a list of best-selling books,
both fiction and non-fiction. Interest in which
books sell the most copies has been a long-standing
American tradition. In fact, the nation's first best-
seller appeared in 1664. Entitled *A Call to the
Unconverted,* it was written by Richard Baxter, a
celebrated British Puritan preacher and writer. Such
early books are housed in university libraries and
museums and seldom come up for sale. However,
there's plenty of opportunity to begin a rare book
collection. One way is to purchase books of current
authors you feel will have lasting value as writers.
If you select the right authors, you might see sizeable profits in years to come.

   If you decide to collect modern first editions,
keep in mind that works of unknown authors are

If you begin to collect rare books you will need to understand these special terms:

As issued: The original condition of volume.

Association copy: A copy that belonged to the author or to a person whose relationship with the author or the book's contents bears an interesting association.

Broadside: Printing done on only one side of a sheet of paper.

Editio princeps: The Latin phrase used by antiquarians for "first edition."

Errata: When errors are discovered after printing, often a separate sheet is added after the binding to list these mistakes for the reader.

Ex-library: Any book that has been in a lending library.

Foxed, foxing: Paper stained or discolored, usually from age.

Leaf: Sheet of paper containing a front and back page—the single production unit.

Provenance: Ownership history of a book, traced in a variety of ways, which often provides an interesting sidelight to owning a particular copy of a rare book.

Re-backed: A book that has been given a new spine or strip along the back to secure the front and back covers.

Sophisticated: A euphemistic term for a book that has had pages added or replaced from other copies.

Variants: A copy of a particular edition that is noticeably different from other copies because of misprints, changes made during printing, or other factors.

usually printed in small quantities. Then, if the author's book becomes a top seller, the publisher will go back to press and print additional copies. However, only that first batch are true first editions. This happened with Larry McMurtry's Pulitzer Prize-winning book, *Lonesome Dove,* published in 1985 at $18.95. A year later it was worth $50 because the publisher miscalculated demand and didn't print many copies.

Guidelines to keep in mind:

1) Buy only hard-cover books. Paperback and book club editions have no value as collectibles.

2) Look for the words "first edition" on the copyright page, which follows the title page.

3) To assure yourself of getting a true first edition, buy an author's books when they are first published. Don't wait six months.

4) Autographed first editions can be worth 100 percent more than unsigned first editions.

5) Save the dust jacket. To preserve it in mint condition, use a plastic cover, such as those used by libraries.

6) Never mark in the book. Don't even write you name.

As your collection grows, keep a detailed index of your holdings. You may want to insure your collection under your parents' homeowners insurance policy. Keep your list in a separate location and update it annually. Good records are useful in substantiating an insurance claim if your collection is damaged or destroyed.

First editions can be found at ordinary bookstores, such as Waldenbooks and B. Dalton, as well as at independent booksellers and second-hand stores. Antiquarian bookstores are another source for first editions, but prices are usually higher. Turn to these stores when selling or when seeking a specific title.

The difficult question, of course, is which books or authors to buy. With thousands of books being published every year, the choices are endless. Trust your judgment or that of someone who is knowledgeable about modern authors, but be sure to keep in mind that good writing will usually endure the test of time. Don't be afraid to speculate in new, young writers.

Ideas for Specializing
- Books of one author
- Books on a favorite topic
- Children's books
- Old school books

For More Information
- Libraries to Contact:
  The Pierpont Morgan Library
  Madison Avenue at 36th Street
  New York, NY 10016
  212-685-0610

  Rare Book Collection
  New York Public Library
  Fifth Avenue at 42nd Street
  New York, NY 10018
  212-930-0800

- To check what a book is worth,
  refer to these guides, available
  in public libraries and many
  antique shops:
  American Book Prices Current.
  Washington, CT:
  Bancroft-Parkman Inc., annual
  *Bookman's Price Index: A
  Guide to the Values of Rare and
  Out-of-Print Books,* Daniel F.
  McGrath, editor. Detroit, MI:
  Gale Research; 1964 to date;
  annual.

- To find a reliable dealer:
  Send a self-addressed #10
  envelope with 65 cents postage
  to:
  Antiquarian Bookseller's
  Association
  50 Rockefeller Plaza
  New York, NY 10020
  212-757-9395

- Magazines:
  The Armchair Detective
  129 West 56th Street
  New York, NY 10019
  212-765-0902 (0900?)
  Quarterly; $26 a year
     This quarterly has a column
  that focuses on one mystery
  author in each issue, and tells
  where to find that person's
  book, the price range, and how
  to judge condition, etc.

- For information on small presses:
  Fine Print
  P.O. Box 193394
  San Francisco, CA 94107
  415-543-4455

Bottles

If you live in an old house, go out the back door and
take about five long strides straight ahead and then
three or four steps to the left or right. That's where

you're likely to find bottles that were buried in the old days before the garbage truck made its weekly rounds.

Collecting bottles is both easy and fun. Other inexpensive sources besides the backyard are old hotel sales, dumps and junk yards, second-hand stores, and thrift shops.

Glass blowing and bottle-making goes back to ancient times, but America revolutionized the process around the 1780s when a glassblower in New England made the first free-blown bottle without seams. Because these bottles were blown without the use of a mold, no two bottles from this period are exactly alike. Later on, seams appeared again and today's machine-made bottles have a mold seam running up the side of the bottle. After free-blown bottles, glassblowers refined their skills to do pattern molding. This allowed the bottle to be blown with a raised pattern on it. Pattern molding can double the value.

Ideas for Specializing

There are more than one hundred different types of bottles. Here are some choices for building a collection.

• *Carboys and Demijohns.* Made to hold vinegar, cider, and applejack, they are narrow-necked, and light green with no decoration.

• *Flasks and Whiskey Bottles.* Flasks are flat-sided and were originally used to carry gunpowder and then, later on, liquor. Some have presidential portraits on them.

• *Bitters and Patent Medicines.* Manufactured between 1820 and 1905, these come in a variety of sizes and shapes, although most are square, rectangular or hexagonal.

• *Fruit Jars.* Before 1860, fruits and vegetables were preserved by drying them. Around the time of the Civil War, the Mason screw-top jar appeared on the market. These jars, with their thick glass and sturdy appearance, became the model for other storage jars.

• *Ink Bottles.* Small, conical or pyramidal in shape, these are quite beautiful. Larger ink bottles, with cylindrical containers and a pinched pouring spout, are rarer than smaller ones.

• *Poison Bottles.* In the 1800s there was a law passed requiring poison bottles to have ridges on them so they could be felt in the dark. In the 1900s, however, the law was eliminated because they found children were attracted to the ridged bottles.

• *Cosmetic Bottles.* Perfume or cologne bottles were usually sealed with ground-glass stoppers and decorated with beaded-rope designs. Hair tonic bottles also fell into this grouping. In addition to historical bottles, more recent perfume bottles are becoming collectibles. These include Prince Matchabelli, Hattie Carnegie, Lalique, and Baccarat. You should also start saving any of today's uniquely designed, decorative bottles.

For More Information
• Museums to Contact:
  The Bennington Museum
  West Main Street
  Bennington, VT 05201
  802-447-1571

The Corning Museum of Glass
1 Museum Way
Corning, NY 14830
607-937-5371

Toledo Museum of Art
2445 Monroe Street
Toledo, OH 43697
419-255-8000

• Clubs and Organizations:
  The Federation of Historical
  Bottles Club
  14521 Atlantic
  Riverdale, IL 60627
  708-841-4068

• Magazines:
  *Antique Bottle and Glass
  Collector*
  Box 187
  East Greenville, PA 18041
  215-679-5849
  Monthly; $16 per year

• Books:
  Kovel's Bottles Price List by
  Ralph and Terry Kovel. New
  York: Crown, 1987.
  A Treasury of American Bottles
  by William C. Ketchum, Jr.
  New York: The Bobbs-Merrill
  Company, Inc., 1975.

Coins
Metal tokens from the past often fetch big prices in the present. King Croesus, the legendary ruler of the ancient kingdom of Lydia, launched the world

into coinmaking and collecting more than 2,500 years ago when he **minted** the first-known silver coin. The rulers of Babylonia, Greece, Turkey, and Rome also authorized their own coins, often stamped with their portrait on one side and their heraldic emblem on the other. Thus, royalty became the world's first coin dealers.

Minted: The process of making coins. Coins are struck at a mint, under the auspices of the government.

Today an estimated 20 million Americans collect coins. Some have made money, but none have become as "rich as Croesus," although several years ago an 1804 United States silver dollar went for $900,000. But that's the exception, not the rule.

Rare coins fall into five basic groups: ancient, classic foreign, early United States, modern foreign and American **Commemoratives,** minted to mark historic events, are considered rare, too. The value of these coins is determined not just by their condition but by their scarcity and collector appeal.

Commemoratives: Coins issued in honor of an event or person.

Numismatic coins are either circulated or uncirculated. Generally, uncirculated coins are more valuable. In other words, a coin is more valuable if it looks the same as when it was minted. Collectors call these Mint State (MS) or Uncirculated (Unc.). Business-strike coins, used in our everyday life, are called circulated coins.

Numismatics: The study or collecting of coins, tokens, medals, and paper money.

If you decide to collect coins, read one of the guidebooks listed below before beginning. One is likely to encounter more dishonesty in this field than in many of the others discussed in this book. And, unfortunately, fakes, forgeries, and promises of great deals are not uncommon. As you assemble a collection, keep in mind that any visible flaw, hairline scratch, nick, abrasion, even smooth spots due to wear, can mean a big difference in value. Perfection is found only in proofs, mirrorlike coins intended solely for collectors and investors. They are stamped twice at the Mint for extra clear image.

In an effort to standardize grading coins, the nonprofit American Numismatic Association established a numerical system, dividing circulated and uncirculated into 24 grades. The lowest circulated grade is Poor-I; the highest is Very Choice. The lowest uncirculated grade is MS-60, while the highest is MS-70.

The current prices of gold and silver **bullion** also influence the value of coins, such as the American Eagle, Canadian Maple Leaf, South African Krugerrand, Mexican 50 Peso, Australian Nugget, Austrian Corono, and British Sovereign. These coins tend to trade at a percentage above the **spot price** of the metal.

Bullion: Gold or silver as raw material, or ingots before made into coins.

Spot price: The cash price for a commodity such as gold or silver.

Ideas for Specializing

Begin by collecting money used in the United States, such as early pennies, the $20 gold St. Gaudens, all 50 U.S. silver commemoratives, the $5 or $2.50 Indian gold pieces, and the Morgan Silver dollars.

For More Information
• Clubs and Organizations:
  American Numismatic
  Association

818 North Cascade Avenue
Colorado Springs, CO 80903
800-367-9723

The International Numismatic Society
P.O. Box 66555
Washington, DC 20035
202-223-4496

• To find a dealer in your area,
  contact:
  The American Numismatic
  Association (see above)

The Numismatic Society &
Museum
617 West 155th Street
New York, NY 10032
212-234-3130

The Professional Numismatists
Guild
P.O.Box 430
Van Nuys, CA 91408
818-781-1764
(Offers a brochure, "What You
Should Know Before You Buy
Rare Coins For Investment.")

• Magazines:
Coin World
Amos Press
P.O.Box 150
Sidney, OH 45365
513-498-0800
Monthly; $26 per year

Numismatic World
Krause Publications
700 East State Street
Iola, WI 54990
715-445-2214
Monthly; $24.95 per year

• Books:
*Complete Encyclopedia of
United States Coins* by Walter
Breen. New York: Doubleday,
1988.

*Consumer Alert: Investing in
Rare Coins;* free from: Federal
Trade Commission, Information
Services, Room B3, Sixth Street
and Pennsylvania Ave., NW,
Washington, DC 20580.

*A Consumer's Guide to Coin
Investment;* free from:
Blanchard & Co., Box 61740,
New Orleans, LA 70161-1740.

A Guide to United States Coins
by R.S. Yeoman. Racine, WI:
Western Publishing Co., 1990.

Comic Books

Some of your favorite comic book characters have
been around a long time. Most experts regard F.M.
Howarth's *Funny Folks,* issued in 1899, as the first
true American comic book. For years afterwards,
comic books were issued in a number of different
sizes and formats. Then, in 1933, the comic book
was standardized when Max Gaines produced

Funnies on Parade, the first modern comic book. Five years later, in June 1938, the most successful comic character of all time, Superman, made his debut in *Action Comics #1.* Since then at least 80,000 different comics have been issued.

If you decide to build a collection, keep in mind that comic books must be in good condition to have value as a collectible. And, the older the better, with the classics commanding the best prices. These include names familiar to all of us: Mickey Mouse, Donald Duck, Popeye, Superman, Batman, and Captain Marvel.

For More Information

• Magazines:
    Comic Buyer's Guide
    Krause Publications, Inc.
    700 East State Street
    Iola, WI 54990
    715-445-2214
    Weekly; $27.95 per year

• Books
    The Official Overstreet Comic Book Price Guide by Robert M. Overstreet. New York: Ballantine Books, 1990.

Comic Strips

The daily newspaper comic strip is also a truly American form of art. Among the early examples of daily or Sunday comic strips that are popular with collectors are Terry and the Pirates, Krazy Kat, Popeye, Flash Gordon, Buster Brown, Steve Canyon, Prince Valiant, Tarzan, and Little Nemo. Contemporary strips to consider are Peanuts, Hagar the Horrible, Calvin and Hobbes, L'il Abner, Pogo, and The Far Side.

In the early days, each individual drawing was done by the artist in pen and ink. If they were to appear in the Sunday paper in color, they were either color coded or colored by artists working for the individual newspapers. The ones that are most prized are the original black and white drawings, not the colored, photostated versions.

The number of times the original character appears in the strip, the appearance of another key character, and the condition of the panel are all factors in determining a comic strip's value. Generally, the earlier the strip, the more valuable it is.

Ideas for Specializing
- One character
- Disney publications
- Books by a certain artist
- In foreign languages

For More Information
- Museums to Contact:
  The Cartoon Museum
  4300 S. Semoran Blvd.
  Orlando, FL 32822
  407-273-0141

  Museum of Cartoon Art
  Comly Avenue
  Rye Brook, NY 10573
  914-939-0234

- Clubs and Organizations:
  The Mouse Club (for Disney collectors)
  2056 Cirone Way
  San Jose, CA 95124
  408-377-2590

- Books:
  Collecting Comic Books by Marcia Leiter. Boston: Little Brown & Co., 1983.

  The Official Overstreet Comic Book Price Guide Companion by Robert M. Overstreet. New York: Ballantine Books, 1989.

Dolls

Dolls, along with stamps and coins, are one of the world's most popular collectibles. One reason for their appeal is that they tell the history of different peoples. For instance, many ancient cultures, such as those of Egypt, Mesopotamia, Persia, India, and Greece, used dolls as religious symbols and often as companions in death.

Collectors divide dolls into several periods as explained in the box on page 97. Today, however, most concentrate on dolls from the "Golden Age of

Dollmaking," which lasted from 1875 to 1925, and on "Modern Dolls," of 1920-1950.

The dolls collectors prize most today are those made of bisque between the years 1875 and 1925. The leading manufacturers were Leon Bru and Pierre Jumeau—both French; and two Germans: Kestner and Armand Marseille. The second most popular type are celebrity dolls from the 1930s and 1940s, particularly Shirley Temples, Mary Pickfords, and Sonja Henies. Regardless of the type or manufacturer, a doll is always more valuable when it's wearing its original clothes. Other features that add to value: rarity, age, excellent condition, detailed workmanship, an unusual size, a fascinating history, and one with its original box.

The earliest manufactured American dolls were turned out by Ludwig Greiner, a German immigrant who lived in Philadelphia. He won a patent in 1858 for papier- mâché dolls backed with linen. Dolls made by Izannah Walker of Central Falls, Rhode Island, around 1860 are also highly prized. Other early commercially made American dolls sought by collectors are those made by four Springfield, Vermont, manufacturers: The Co-operative Manufacturing Co., D.M. Smith & Co., H.H. Mason, and The Jointed Doll Co. They all made wooden dolls that today are known as "Springfields."

Special terms

In order to develop your doll collection, you will need to know these terms.

Ball-joint: When balls of wood or other material are attached to sockets of a doll's limbs in order to allow the limbs to move.

Barbie doll: First manufactured by Mattel Toys in 1959.

Bebé : French dolls representing small children up to about age 7.

Bisque: Unglazed porcelain, usually tinted with a dull rather than a glossy patina. Used for heads and sometimes for bodies.

Bonnet bisques: Bisque-headed dolls decorated with bisque hats. Often flowers and bows were molded in as part of the head itself.

Boudoir dolls: Not designed for children to play with but to be used as bedroom decorations by women. Popular in the 1920s; made until the 1940s.

Celebrity dolls: Dolls created in the likeness of famous people.

Character dolls: Realistic-looking dolls as opposed to dolls representing idealized conceptions of children. Character dolls date from about 1909.

China-heads: Dolls made of glazed porcelain. Bodies are often of cloth.

Composition: A combination of materials, such as sawdust or wood pulp with glue, that is molded into bodies and heads and then allowed to harden.

Eyes, flirty: Doll eyes that move from side to side and sometimes up and down.

Eyes, googly: Eyes that look to the side. Also called "goo-goo" or "rougish" eyes.

Eyes, intaglio: Painted-on eyes as opposed to inset glass ones.

Frozen Charlotte: A one-piece, immobile doll named after an 1860s song about a girl who wanted

- 1840-1880: Hand-carved, woooden dolls are phased out and new materials are developed: wax, china (glazed porcelain), and parian (fine, lightly glazed porcelain). Mass distribution begins with England, France and Germany the leading manufacturers. American dolls of this period are mainly hand-made from cloth or papier-mache.

- 1870: Bisque, an unglazed, matte ceramic, is introduced. Heads of bisque are appealing because they look like human skin.

- 1880: The French, leaders of the doll inductry until the turn of the century, begin mass production of bisque "bebe" luxury dolls for children. Dressed in expensive designer costumes, bebes reflect the Victorian ideal of children as miniature adults who were rarely seen and seldom heard.

- 1880-1899: Germans take the lead. Bisque remains the most popular material.

- 1900-1915: The psychological theories of Freud and Jung influence dolls as German factories create more realistic looking dolls whose faces are no longer bland but have character, and therefore are called "character dolls." The most famous such firm was Kammer & Reinhardt, known to collectors as "K*R." A K*R recently sold at auction for $47,000.

- 1910: America becomes prominent in the doll market, successfully competing with European manufacturers. Schoenhut of Philadelphia makes wooden dolls and Fulper Pottery Works of New Jersey turns out ceramic dolls.

- 1925-1940: Bisque is surpassed by "composition," a combination of clays, fibers, sawdust and other materials. Until World War II, the U.S. dominates the world doll market.

- 1945: Doll manufacturing is revolutionized by the introduction of plastics.

to show off her new dress. She dashed out into the cold without a coat and was frozen stiff.

Kewpie dolls: Elfin-like dolls, usually of all bisque, created in the early twentieth century by Rose O'Neill, an actress who became a magazine illustrator. She drew a pixie-like cupid (hence,

"Kewpie") and in 1909 wrote a story about this character. By 1913 Kewpie dolls appeared in a great many magazines. A successor is the Barbie doll.

Lady dolls: Dolls constructed to represent an adult female.

Name dolls: Dolls bearing manufacturer-assigned names, such as the Shirley Temple doll and the Madame Alexander "Little Women" dolls.

Open-mouth: A mouth with parted lips, with an opening into the head.

Papier-mâché: A mixture of paper pulp, glue, and starch.

Parian: Dolls made of untinted bisque, with the features and hair being the only areas of color. The word "Parian" comes from the Greek *Paros,* a city noted for its fine, pale marble.

Peddlers: Dolls, usually dating from the nineteenth or early twentieth century, that hold trays brimming over with miniatures of wares for sale. Peddlers were made of a variety of materials, including bisque, kid, and papier mache. Those in their original glass domes are particularly valuable.

Peg wooden: A carved doll of solid wood with face and shoes painted on.

Rag doll: A doll made entirely of cloth; also called a cloth doll.

Springfield doll: A jointed wooden doll made in Springfield, Vermont.

Waxed: A papier maché, composition, or wooden doll that is coated with wax.

Ideas for Specializing

- Oriental dolls
- French bebes
- French lady dolls
- Celebrity dolls
- Bride and groom sets
- China dolls
- Black bisque dolls
- Character dolls

- Military dolls
- Barbie dolls
- Hand-made dolls

For Further Information
- Museums to Contact:
  The Washington Dolls' House
  and Toy Museum
  5236 44th Street N.W.
  Washington, DC 20015
  202-244-0024

- Clubs and Organization:
  Doll Collectors of America
  14 Chestnut Street
  Westford, MA 01886
  508-692-8392

- Magazines:
  The Dollmasters Newsletter
  Theriault's
  Box 151
  Annapolis, MD 21401
  301-224-3655
  Quarterly; $9 per year

- Books:
  The ABCs of Doll Collecting by
  John C. Schweitzer. New York:
  Sterling Publishing Co., Inc., 1981.

  The Doll Registry by Florence
  Theriault. (A price guide and
  reference work) Annapolis:
  Theriault's, 1989.

Games

The ancient Sumerians were among the first to make games that we know about. But, of course, these and all other ancient games are very expensive. However, more recent games, such as jigsaw puzzles, are much more reasonably priced. A London painter, John Spilsbury, created the modern jigsaw puzzle in 1762 while looking for a way to market his engraved maps. He came up with the idea of gluing the maps to thin cedar and mahogany panels, which were then cut into sections. They were reassembled by children as an educational tool.

The first American board games were produced by the W. & S.B. Ives Company of Salem, Massachusetts. In 1843 this company produced "Mansion of Happiness," in which the different squares penalize sin and reward righteousness. This game pioneered the basic linear format in which players follow a prearranged course drawn on the board up until the end. Ives's first games were printed on cardboard and hand-colored by women working on an assembly line, each one filling in a color.

Another early American manufacturer was McLoughlin Brothers, Inc., a New York company that issued games, toys, and children's books from the 1850s until it was absorbed by Milton Bradley Co. in 1920. Bradley published its first game, "The Checkered Game of Life," in 1860. By 1882 this Springfield, Massachusetts, company employed over 500 people and was producing 400 games, puzzles and other playthings.

In 1920, Parker Brothers, by then already a leading board game manufacturer, introduced a new parlor game played not on a board but on a table divided by a net. It was a version of table tennis but instead of an India rubber, the ball was made of celluloid. The sound that this light plastic ball made when it was hit led to its name: ping pong. Eventually a larger table was used, but the first version is now a collector's item.

Games tend to follow our national enthusiasms. For instance, when baseball first became an official game, a version was boxed as a game. The George A. Childs Company of Brattleboro, Vermont introduced "The Game of Football" in 1895 when college football was the rage.

Ideas for Specializing
- Chess sets
- Parlor games
- Foreign games
- Playing cards
- Games by a certain manufacturer
- Board games
- Panoramas and dioramas
- Children's games
- Puzzles

For Further Information
- Museums to Contact:
  Museum of the City of New York
  1220 Fifth Avenue
  New York, NY 10029
  212-534-1672

Holiday Collectibles

National and religious holidays have given rise to a number of relatively inexpensive collectibles. The key categories are described below. You can also collect Halloween, Fourth of July, and Easter memorabilia, as well as noisemakers.

New Year's Cards

The ancient Egyptians and Romans exchanged small tokens on New Year's Day—fruits, olive branches, flowers, feathers, and lucky copper coins—all of which symbolized friendship. These symbols were also pictured on tablets and medals, accompanied by a holiday greeting. Two such New Year's medals, addressed to the Emperor Hadrian, who reigned from A.D.117 to 138 , still exist. They have a portrait of the emperor on one side and on the other the message: "The Senate and the People of Rome wish a Happy and Prosperous New Year to Hadrianus Augustus, the father of the country."

Although New Year's greetings were undoubtedly popular in other ancient civilizations, there are no remaining examples until about 1450, when the Germans produced ready-made greeting cards. From 1450 and up until the 16th century, New Year's cards were woodcuts. Thereafter, these cards were produced in many countries, including America.

Christmas

• *Christmas cards.* People first began mailing Christmas cards to their friends in the early 19th century. Credit for the idea is attributed to Henry Cole, who commissioned a friend, Calcott Horsley of the Royal Academy in London, to design a Christmas card for Cole to send to friends. In 1881, Christmas cards were produced in great numbers by the De LaRue Company, an English publishing

house. Another famous commercial English artist of the 19th century was Kate Greenway. She is known in particular for her beautifully drawn children. For many years she was associated with Marcus Ward & Co. of London. In the 1860s, Louis Prang, a German immigrant, fostered the production of Christmas cards in America. He attracted the country's leading artists by sponsoring open competitions for designs and giving large cash prizes to the winners.

Look for early hand-made cards, religious, three-dimensional, colored lithographs, frosted cards, joke or trick cards and cards for children.

• *Christmas decorations.* Hand-made and commercially manufactured ornaments for Christmas trees are relatively easy to find. The first

Christmas trees appeared in this country around 1819, but were rather rare until later in the century. Initially trees were decorated with edibles, such as cookies, fruit, and nuts. Then, in the 1860s, German immigrants brought with them the first glass ornaments—icicles and heavy glass balls. By 1870, these ornaments were commercially imported from a small German village called Lauscha, a glass blowing- center of Europe. During World War I, because of the embargo on German-made products, American companies began producing ornaments.

Valentines

According to legend, Valentines are a tribute to St. Valentine, an ancient martyred Roman priest. The story goes that when Claudius the Cruel issued a decree forbidding marriage, this priest defied the ruling. In fact, he was dragged away from the altar while conducting a wedding ceremony and thrown into prison where he died, some say on February 14th. Soon thereafter he became the patron saint of lovers.

The earliest known Valentine dates back to 1415 and was sent by Charles, Duke of Orleans and a prisoner in the tower of London, to his wife. Experts disagree as to the exact year of the first commercial Valentine. Some say 1761; others, 1819. Regardless, the tradition was popular by the 19th century. The workmanship and design of both the Valentine and the envelope from this period are extremely fine. Many have intricate lace patterns. The Victorians created even more elaborate designs through embossing, engraving, and lithography. They also loved sachet Valentines—perfumed cotton was sewn into a small satin pillow, which was wrapped in lacy paper. Other examples included artificial flowers that required special boxes for mailing. In the 1890s, the Germans introduced mechanical cards—three-dimensional pull-outs.

The first American to publish commercial Valentines was Esther A. Howland. She launched her business in 1847, the year she graduated from Mount Holyoke College. She called her firm Howland's New England Valentine Co. Howland initially conceived the idea for her company from a Valentine sent from England to her father in Worcester, Massachusetts. She hoped to sell $5 worth the first year; but much to her surprise, she rang up $5,000 in sales. Thereafter she hired a number of women to assemble bits of ribbon, lacy papers and colored pictures and turn them into Valentines.

Mother's Day Cards

You may think that Mother's Day is a relatively new celebration. However, we know that on one Sunday each year, the young apprentices in 17th century Europe went "a-mothering," unless they were working too far from home to visit on that day. In that case, they sent greetings by letter to their mothers.

Ideas for Specialization
- By holiday
- By age group
- Religious subjects
- By character (Santa Claus, Baby Jesus, Cupid, Easter Bunny)
- By country
- Mechanical cards
- By material

For Further Information
- Museums to Contact:
  New York Historical Society
  170 Central Park West
  New York, NY 10024
  212-873-3400

- Clubs and Organizations:
  National Valentine Collectors' Association
  Box 1404
  Santa Ana, CA 92702
  714-547-1355

• Magazines:

Paper Collectors' Marketplace
470 Main Street
Scandinavia, WI 54977
715-467-2379
Monthly; $15.95 per year

National Valentine Collectors Bulletin
The Association (see page 104)
Quarterly; $16

• Books:

Complete Book of Paper Antiques by Adelaide Hechtlinger and Wilbur Cross. New York: Coward McCann, 1972.

The Christmas Tree Book by Phillip V. Snyder; New York: Penguin, 1976.

Jewelry

In 1949, thousands of American women gave Carol Channing a standing ovation night after night as she belted out the song, "Diamonds Are a Girl's Best Friend" in the play *Gentlemen Prefer Blondes.* They were right, at least from an investment point of view. In fact, not only are diamonds a girl's best friend, but so are rubies, emeralds, sapphires, and even jewelry without fancy expensive stones—if it's good-quality estate jewelry that once adorned the ears, neck, fingers, and arms of someone else.

Older jewelry, sold at estate sales, is often reasonable in price and usually less expensive than new pieces from Tiffany's, Cartier's, and other jewelry stores. If it has a known provenance, the chance of its escalating in price is excellent. The sale of the Duchess of Windsor's jewelry at an auction in 1987, for instance, brought $50 million.

You don't have to shop in the same price category as the Windsor jewels. Here are the factors that contribute to a smart buy in estate jewelry:

• Provenance: If a piece was owned by someone famous, it is almost always worth more.

• Age is an advantage.

• The better the quality and condition, the better the investment.

- The stones should be well cut.
- The signature of the maker or designer adds value.

Very little jewelry survived antiquity and that which did is beyond our price range or is in famous collections and museums. For the average collector, jewelry collecting generally begins with the Georgian era, or at the early part of the 18th century. The subsequent eras, known as the Victorian, Edwardian, art nouveau, and art deco periods, also produced a great many pieces. Newer pieces, so-called retro items, big clunky pieces, and well-made costume jewelry are also collectibles. Bakelite jewelry—Depression-era bracelets and necklaces in brightly colored enamel that were sold at the five and ten—is currently the rage.

Ideas for Specializing
- By designer
- By stone/material
- By era
- By type

For Further Information
- Best Museum for Costume Jewelry is:
  Victoria & Albert
  London, England

Marbles

This ancient game, played in England as long as 400 years ago, may not be as popular as it once was, yet individual round spheres, or, "marbles" used to play the game have become a much sought after collectible. Marbles measure 1/2 to 1 1/2 inches in diameter, but interestingly, are seldom made of marble! The antique ones, which are especially valuable, are made of glass, steel, porcelain, clay, and even semiprecious stones, including agate, onyx, rose quartz, and carnelian. Most antique marbles were hand-made before World War I in Germany, although there were factories in other countries, including the United States. Since the

Second World War, American marbles have been mass-produced by machine and the those of interest to collectors are comic marbles—those that have faces or heads of comic strip characters on them.

The value of a marble depends on the material, its beauty, and design. Sulphides, which have animal or human figures sculpted out of gypsum or clay and then embedded within a glass body, are among the most valuable.

Another favorite are those made of a special kind of goldstone, glass flecked with golden, shining copper particles. Look for Lutz goldstones, named after the French-born designer Nicholas Lutz, who worked at the Boston & Sandwich Glass Co. of Massachusetts during the late 19th century.

Another type of collectible marble is called "balls." These are larger than regular marbles but smaller than bowling balls. They were made of glazed porcelain in the 19th century for a popular game called bowls, played on a rug or the lawn.

Whether you play or collect marbles, here are the words you will run into:

Aggie: A slightly larger than average marble, often of agate. Also called a flint or an agate.

Bowl: A large ball, sometimes 5 inches in diameter, used for bowling games. Also called a carpet ball.

Bumboozer: A large agate or glass marble used as a shooter when playing the game.

Candy: An early German glass marble with a solid swirl of color in the middle.

Chalkie: A marble of clay, limestone, or gypsum; unglazed.

China: A porcelain marble, usually decorated. Also called a chiny.

Clambroth: A milky white marble with thin swirls inside.

Clearie: A clear glass marble or one made of a translucent solid color.

Commie: A clay marble.

Custard: A marble of pale yellow-orange opaque glass.

End-of-day: A marble made with colored glass crumbs that were left over at the end of the marblemaker's workday.

Glassie: A glass marble, often used as a shooter.

Goldstone: A glass marble containing particles of copper that sparkle like gold.

Joseph swirl: So named because its display of colors is suggestive of the many colors of Joseph's coat as described in the Bible.

Marriiddle: A handmade clay marble.

Mib: A marble, often of clay, used as a target in the game.

Peewee: A very small marble.

Peppermint swirl: Named after the striped Christmas candy.

Pontil mark: A circular nub or bump where a handmade marble was cut off a heated glass rod.

Slag: A marble of solid colored glass, often purple, green, or brown, with wavy lines of white running through it.

Sulphides: Marbles with three-dimensional figures embedded within transparent glass. Figures include animals, famous people, numbers, ships, and trains. Among the most prized of all marbles.

Vaseline: Yellowish-green opaque glass.

For Further Information

• Museums to Contact:

    Children's Museum
    67 East Kirby
    Detroit, MI
    313-494-1210

    Sandwich Glass Museum
    129 Main Street
    Sandwich, MA 02536
    508-888-0251

• Clubs and Organizations:
The Marble Collectors Society of America
P.O. Box 222
Trumbull, CT 06611
203-261-3223

• Books:
Collecting Antique Marbles by Paul Baumann. Wallace-Homestead Book Co., 1970.
The Great America Marble Book by Fred Ferretti. New York: Workman Publishing Co., 1973.

Movie Posters

The rage for old movies has given rise to an affordable collectible—the movie poster. Prices range from $35 to several thousand dollars.

The earliest movie posters seldom dealt with the film at all. Instead, they advertised what was then an exciting new miracle—moving pictures. It wasn't until Thomas Edison's 1897 film, *A Morning Alarm,* that a poster actually showed a scene from the movie it was advertising. By the early years of the 20th century, movie posters had become more sophisticated, showing specific scenes and giving information about the film and the production company. These posters were drawn up by the studios and then sent to printers. Most were designed anonymously and only a limited number were printed. The theater owner would rent posters from the studio to put outside his theater to attract moviegoers. When the run was over, he was able to

HOT MOVIE POSTERS

Gone with the Wind	Casablanca
They Died with Their Boots On	The Winning Team
Annie Hall	The Last Will and
The Big Sleep	Testament of Dr. Mabuse
Arsenic and Old Lace	Return of the Jedi

return the posters to one of many film exchanges throughout the country, where they were either stored or destroyed. Of course, the owners often kept the posters, tossing them in a corner or storing them in a closet. Many were turned in during World War II paper drives.

Although most movie posters were done anonymously, there are several notable exceptions. Those that were signed typically bring higher prices than unsigned ones. Signed posters include Norman Rockwell's designs for *The Razor's Edge*; Saul Bass's posters for *In Harm's Way, Vertigo, Man with the Golden Arm*, and *The Two of Us*; and Milton Glazer's poster for *Next Stop, Greenwich Village*. Al Hirschfeld and Thomas Hart Benton also designed some posters.

Ideas for Specializing
- Famous stars
- Silent films
- Famous producers
- Foreign films

For More Information
- For prices of all types of movie collectibles, consult:
  Hollywood Studio Magazine
  3960 Laurel Canyon Blvd.
  Studio City, CA 91614
  818-990-5450
  Monthly; $25.97 per year

- Museums to Contact:
  Academy of Motion Picture
  Arts and Sciences
  8949 Wilshire Blvd.
  Beverly Hills, CA 90211
  213-278-8990

Museum of Modern Art
11 West 53rd Street
New York, NY 10019
212-708-9400

New York Public Library
Museum of the Performing Arts
Lincoln Center
111 Amsterdam at 65th Street
New York, NY 10023
212-870-1670

- Clubs and Organizations:
  National Association of Paper
  and Advertising Collectors
  P.O. Box 500
  Mount Joy, PA 17552
  717-653-8240

• Magazines:
  Classic Images
  Box 809
  Muscatine IA 52761
  319- 263-2331
  Monthly; $25 per year

• Books:
  Collecting Movie Memorabilia
  by Sol Chaneles. New York:
  Arco Publishing Co., Inc., 1977.

Political Memorabilia

Hold on to those Bush-Quayle and Dukakis-Bentsen buttons. Campaign memorabilia—buttons, banners, and books about the candidates—are often hot items long after the election results are in.

The first official campaign button, from the contest between William McKinley and William Jennings Bryan, appeared in 1896. The most valuable version of these buttons portrays McKinley and his running mate, Garrett Hobart, riding their bikes together up to the White House.

Serious collecting of campaign memorabilia began in the late 1940s in this country and then fell out of favor during the troubled Watergate years. Enthusiasm for this particular type of collectible is always strongest, of course, during election years. Values tend to escalate annually, except in years of political apathy. This was true when Jimmy Carter was in the White House, but Reagan, as a popular movie star turned politician, brought renewed interest to political memorabilia.

Prices are determined by scarcity, demand, desirability, and historical significance. Rare political pieces have advanced dramatically in value while run-of-the-mill pieces just keep pace with inflation.

The easiest way to begin is to gather all of the material from a current campaign. Start with campaign buttons, looking for those with the candidate's pictures and catchy slogans. Buttons with only the candidate's name are turned out by the thousands and have less potential for appreciation.

Autographs, misspellings, pictures, anything unusual, adds to the desirability of a piece.

Caution: In 1968, Amoco and Kleenex produced numerous replicas of historical buttons. Unscrupulous dealers sometimes try to sell them as the real thing. The Hobby Protection Act requires that reproductions must be labeled, but experience is the real key to spotting fakes.

Buttons and banners are not the only valuable and interesting pieces that stand the test of time. First editions of books by and about politicians and signed autographed copies tend to hold their value. You can begin collecting current books by living ex-presidents as well as biographies published about them. Keep in mind that an autographed copy immediately adds to the long-term value of the book. (See Books, page 86.)

For a catalog listing the prices of political books, documents and photographs, contact:

Abraham Lincoln Book Shop
357 West Chicago Ave.
Chicago, IL 60610
312-944-3085

In addition to books, banners, and badges, political collections can be built around plates, flags, snuff boxes, cups, and even dolls. A Grover Cleveland stickpin that sold for about $40 during the 1970s recently went for $125. A political ribbon from the Abraham Lincoln era, worth about $250 ten years ago, is now priced well over $700.

Note: Hake's Americana & Collectibles runs an auction by mail of Americana items and publishes an auction catalog every two months. It pictures 3,000 items (500 of which are political in nature), with estimated values. Bids are taken by mail or telephone. A sample catalog is available for $5. Contact: Hake's Americana & Collectibles, Box 1444, York, PA 17705, 717-848-1333.

Ideas for Specializing
- One political party
- Presidents
- One politician
- Ribbons and banners

For More Information
- Museums to Contact:
  The various presidential librar- ies and birthplaces of the presi- dents have valuable reference material for collectors. For example: Franklin D. Roosevelt Library and Museum in Hyde Park, New York; the Lyndon Baines Johnson Library in Austin, Texas; the Harry S. Truman Library in Independence, Missouri; and the John F. Kennedy Library in Boston, Massachusetts.

- Clubs and Organizations:
  The American Political Items Collectors
  P.O. Box 340339
  San Antonio, TX 78234
  512-655-8277
  This club has 2,700 members nationwide and produces a number of publications, holds meetings, conducts mail

auctions, and sponsors conventions. Even more important, it distributes a list of members so that collectors can trade with one another. The organization gives free estimates to people who send in a picture of their item and a self-addressed stamped envelope.

• Books:
   The Encyclopedia of Political Buttons by Theodore L. Hake; 4 vols.; York, PA: Hake's Americana & Collectibles, 1974-1978.

Postcards

When you receive a postcard from a friend you probably read it, look at the picture, and toss it away. But in the early part of this century, people didn't throw away their postcards. Between 1900 and 1920, collecting picture postcards was a mania for thousands of people. All over America and Europe people pasted them in albums and then put the albums on coffee tables, where they became conversation pieces. Some families built "postcard closets" and gave "postcard parties" at which the evening's entertainment after dinner was looking at the family's postcard collection.

Deltiology: The hobby of collecting postcards.

The mania passed but **deltiology** has not. There are postcard collectors clubs in every state.

The postcard originated in Europe around 1869 to accommodate short messages for businesses. These early postcards were a sort of open letter sent on plain, stiff cardboard issued by the government. Because rates were less than for sealed letters, these business postcards quickly became popular. Soon thereafter, in the 1870s, pictorial images were added to the front. The illustrations for these early cards were almost universally drawings of tourist hotels in Germany, Austria, and Hungary.

The first picture postcard in America appeared in 1873. It was an advertisement issued by a Philadelphia printing company showing a woman, a trumpet, and a flag. The production was so expensive, however, that the postcard movement died for about twenty years. Then, at the Columbian Exposition of 1893, picture postcards of several of the Fair's buildings were sold in vending machines for a nickel each. After the turn of the century and the start of rural free mail delivery, postcards gained great popularity. Those who could afford to travel to Europe sent picture cards to their relatives.

Between 1900 and 1920, Americans took endless numbers of photographs of their families, friends, major events, and even catastrophes, with their Kodak Brownie cameras. These snapshots were printed on special Kodak stock paper with the words "Post Card" on the back. These homemade cards were sent to friends and relatives. Today they are important historical documents of a time.

Linen cards of the 1930s, 1940s, and 1950s issued by hotels, motels, and restaurants are also popular collectibles, as are World War II cards. The most valuable of all cards, however, fall outside most budgets. They are cards by well-known artists, including Toulouse-Lautrec, Mucha, and Bakst.

Hunt for old postcards in your attic, at local flea markets, garage sales, and antique shops.

Ideas for Specializing
- Plants
- Sports
- Animals
- Major Events
- People
- Humor

For More Information
- Museums to Contact:
    Werner and Florence Kent Von Boltenstern's World Wide Postcard Collection
    Loyola Marymount University Library
    Los Angeles, CA 90045
    213-338-2788

• Clubs and Organizations:
 Postcard History Society
 P.O.Box 1765
 Manassas, VA 22110
 703-368-2757

• Magazines:
 Barr's Post Card News
 70 South Sixth Street
 Lansing, Iowa 52151
 319-538-4500
 Weekly; $25 per year

• Books:
 Collector's Guide To Postcards
 by Jane Wood. Paducah, KY:
 Collector Books, 1987.

 The Picture Postcard and Its Origins by Frank Staff. New York: Frederick A. Praeger, Inc., 1966.

Postcard Collecting by Thomas E. Range. New York: E.P. Dutton, 1980.

Postcard Companion: The Collector's Reference by Jack H. Smith. Radnor, PA: Wallace-Homestead Book Co., 1989.

• Dealers:
 For a list of postcard dealers, send a self-addressed business envelope with 45 cents for postage, to:
 International Federation of Postcard Dealers
 P.O.Box 1765
 Manassas, VA 21100
 703-368-2757

Soldiers

People of every age enjoy playing with toy soldiers. And, in fact, many well-known adults have never outgrown the fun of moving miniature soldiers around a battle field: The poet and novelist Robert Louis Stevenson, while recovering from tuberculosis at the age of about 30, played for hours on end with his collection. So too, did Winston Churchill, H.G. Wells, and Douglas Fairbanks, Jr.

Collectors tend to focus on toy soldiers made in Europe and the United States in the 19th and early 20th centuries. These miniatures range in size from about 1 1/4 to 2 1/4 inches and are usually made from an alloy of tin, although some are paper, others are wood, and plaster.

Among the oldest (and most expensive) soldiers are those made in the late 18th century by the German Johann Gottfried Hilpert. They often are marked on the underside with the initials "H," "J.H.," or "J.G.H."

Connoisseur figures, military miniatures never intended for play, appeal to collectors who value historical accuracy. The makers of connoisseur figures researched every detail and duplicated military uniforms down to the last button. The father of connoisseur figures was Richard Courtenay, and English historian and model soldier maker. When he died in 1964, he had created over 300 different models.

At the other end of the price range are paper soldiers, designed to be cut out and pasted on wood or cardboard. Some are beautifully engraved, while others were quickly produced and used as cigarette premiums.

Metal soldiers are especially prized. There are four kinds: flats—two-dimensional and the smallest; semirounds, which are not fully modeled but are rounder than flats; three-dimensional soldiers; and hollow casts, which are three-dimensional, hollow, and lighter in weight than solids. The most desirable of the metal types are the three-dimensionals made by the Parisian firm of Lucotte, the solids made in Germany by Georg Heyde, and the hollow casts produced by W. Britains Ltd., an English firm. Lucotte went into business around 1790 and was taken over by the firm of Henry Mignot in 1875. Many Lucotte soldiers are marked with the initials "L" and "C," flanking the image of a bee. Douglas Fairbanks Jr. at one time had a complete Lucotte 21-man Royal Marine band that cost $1.38 in 1938. In 1977, it was auctioned for almost $1,400.

Among the American manufacturers to look for are McLoughlin Brothers of New York, Barclay Manufacturing Co. of Union City, New Jersey, Manoil Manufacturing Co. of Waverly, New Jersey, and Louis Marx & Co. of New York. Pieces by the latter were sold in the 1941 Montgomery Ward catalog for 98 cents each. Collectors also like the solid Authenticast soldiers, produced by Comet Metal Products during the 1930s and 1940s.

Ideas for Specializing

- By manufacturer
- By country
- By war
- Tanks, trucks and artillery
- Marching bands
- Connoisseur figures
- By material
- By branch of service

For Further Information

- Books:
  Collecting Toy Soldiers by Richard O'Brien. Florence, Alabama: Books Americana, 1988.

Stamps

Stamps are the most popular of all collectibles. The U.S. Post Office estimates that at least 30 million people collect stamps. It is an easy collectible to become involved with and it's also a wonderful way to learn about geography, history, famous people, and even animals and flowers.

It is believed that the Chinese organized the first mail delivery system during the Chou Dynasty. Marco Polo found 10,000 stations with 200,000 horses in the 14th century. Yet as far as we know, stamps were not used until the reign of Queen Victoria, when, in 1840, Rowland Hill conceived of the idea of a stamp as well as a stamped envelope. Today, these early issues are highly prized. In fact, truly rare stamps cost many thousands of dollars, but you can begin for free by collecting stamps on letters and postcards that come to your house or to your parents' places of business. This will introduce you to the variety of current stamps in existence. Then you can branch out by purchasing a packet or bag of mixed stamps. These bags often contain many duplicates but you also end up with several hundred different stamps from all over the world. For a helpful discussion of packets, see Paul Villiard's book *Collecting Stamps*.

Sometimes new collectors think that used stamps do not have the investment potential of mint copies. The experts generally agree that this is a misconception and cite as an example the world's most valuable stamp, the one-cent British Guiana of 1856, which is a used stamp.

Ideas for Specializing
- Airmail stamps
- Souvenir sheets
- Souvenir postcards
- Women on stamps
- Foreign stamps
- First-day covers
- Stamps with errors
- Commemorative stamps

For More Information
- Clubs and Organizations:
  American Philatelic Society
  P.O.Box 8000
  100 Oakwood Avenue
  State College, PA 16803
  814-237-3803

- Books:
  Collecting Stamps by Paul Villiard. New York: Doubleday & Co., 1974.

  Preserving Your Paper Collectibles by Demaris C. Smith. Crozet, VA: Betterway Publications, Inc., 1989.

  Scott Standard Postage Stamp Catalogues. Sidney, OH: Scott Publishing Co., 1991.

  Start Collecting Stamps. Philadelphia, PA: Running Press, 1988.

Trains

Almost every American child has wanted a set of electric trains. Perhaps you already have one and you want to collect more. Most collectors seem to prefer American-made trains. Lionel Trains are ranked number one. Other popular makers are American Flyer, Ives, and Boucher.

There are two distinct periods in train collecting: the classic period, which covers the 1920s until the early 1940s, and the post-World War II period, from 1946 to today, also known as the "plastic era." The first electric trains were made just before the

turn of the century. In 1902, the Lionel Manufacturing Company, was founded by Joshua Lionel
Cowen, was founded. The pre-World War II trains
were heavy, made with brass, and, frequently, tin
plate. Some of the engines weighed as much as 25
pounds and were 30 inches long. After the war,
when plastic was introduced, trains became smaller
and lighter.

There are many off-beat trains to look for. In
1957, the Lionel Train Company sold the Lady
Lionel, a pastel train set for girls. Other colored
trains have appeared over the years: in 1930, Lionel
introduced the Blue Comet. Each car was named
after a comet—Faye, Westphal, Temple. Sears sold
the "Halloween General" in the mid-1950s; it had a
red and black engine and blue cars.

Look for trains in excellent condition, preferably in a boxed set. Most trains are sold at "train
meets" that take place all over the country. The
largest one is in York, Pennsylvania.

Ideas for Specializing
- By era
- By manufacturer
- By color
- By size

For More Information
- Museums to Contact:

Lincoln Train Museum
425 Steinwehr Avenue
Gettysburg, PA 17325
717-334-5678

Toy Train Museum
Paradise Lane
Strasburg, PA 17579
717-687-8976

122

• Clubs and Organizations:
  Train Collectors Association
  P.O. Box 248
  Strasburg, PA 17579
  717-687-8623

• Books:
  *All Aboard! The Story of
  Joshua Lionel Cowen and His
  Lionel Train Company* by Ron
  Hollander. New York: Work-
  man Publishing, 1981.

*Greenberg's Guide to Lionel
Trains* (2 volumes), 1989.
Greenberg Publishing Co., 7566
Main Street, Sykesville, MD
21784; 301-795-7447.

Uncommon Collectibles

There are many other items to consider collecting.
A partial list appears below, with an association or
club to contact for more material on the topic.

• *Antique Pens*
  Pen Fanciers Club
  1169 Overcash Drive
  Dunedin, FL 34698
  813-734-4742

• *Baby Bottles*
  The American Collectors of
  Infant Feeders
  5161 West 59th Street
  Indianapolis, IN 46254
  317-291-5850

• *Bottle Openers*
  Figural Bottle Openers
  Collectors Club
  c/o Barbara Rosen
  6 Shoshone Trail
  Wayne, NJ 07040
  201-835-9330

• *Cookie Cutters*
  Cookie Cutter Collectors Club
  5426 27th Street, NW
  Washington, DC 20015
  202-966-0869

• *Fishing Lures*
  National Fishing Lure
  Collectors Club
  P.O. Box 1791
  Dearborn, MI 48121
  313-842-2589

• *Hand Tools*
  Early American Industries
  Association
  Box 2128
  Empire State Plaza Station
  Albany, NY 12220

• *Hatpins*
  International Club for
  Collectors of Hatpins
  15237 Chanera Avenue
  Gardena, CA 90249
  213-329-2619

• *Hubcaps*
  The Hubcappers
  P.O. Box 54
  Buckley, MI 49620
  616-269-3555

• *Inkwells*
  The Society of Inkwell
  Collectors
  5136 Thomas Avenue South
  Minneapolis, MN 54410
  612-922-2792

• *Maps*
  Chicago Map Society
  c/o Newberry Library
  60 West Walton Street
  Chicago, IL 60610
  312-943-9090

• *Money*
  Society of Paper Money
  Collectors
  P.O. Box 1085
  Florissant, MO 63031

• *Newspapers*
  Newspaper Collectors Society
  of America
  P.O. Box 19134
  Lansing, MI 48901
  517-372-8381

• *Playing Cards*
  Playing Card Collectors
  1559 West Pratt Blvd.
  Chicago, IL 60626
  312-274-0250

• *Quilts*
  American Quilters Society
  P.O. Box 3290
  Paducah, KY 42001
  502-898-7903

• *Salt Cellars*
  The New England Society of
  Open Salt Collectors
  P.O. Box 2007
  Wolfeboro, NH 03894-2007
  603-569-5553

• *Spark Plugs*
  Spark Plug Collectors of
  America
  Box 2229
  Ann Arbor, MI 48106
  313-994-3101

• *Stock & Bond Certificates*
  R.M. Smythe and Company
  26 Broadway
  New York, NY 10004
  212-943-1880

• *Toothpick Holders*
  National Toothpick Holder
  Collectors' Society
  P.O.Box 204
  Eureka, IL 61530
  309-467-2535

INDEX

ACKNOWLEDGEMENTS AND PHOTO CREDITS

Page 2: Lucia Woods/Photo Researchers Inc.; p.8: Robert A. Isaacs/Photo Researchers Inc.; pp. 13,40: Renee Lynn/ Photo Researchers Inc.; p.14: Richard Hutchings/Photo Researchers Inc.; p.17: Jerry Berndt/Stock Boston; pp. 19, 45: UPI/Bettmann Newsphotos; p.20: Margot Granitas/Photo Researchers Inc.; p.27: George Bellerose/ Stock Boston; p.33: Southern Living/Photo Researchers Inc.; pp.39, 102, 103: The Bettmann Archive; pp. 43, 72, 78, 88, 105, 115, 119: Private Collection; p.46: Frank Siteman/Stock Boston; p.53: by Henry Salem Hubbell, The National Portrait Gallery; p.54: Teri Leigh Stratford /Photo Researchers Inc.; p.60: Donald Dietz/Stock Boston; p.90: Courtesy Stcks Coin Company, New York; p.95: Patricia Hollander Gross/Stock Boston; p.98: Peter Vandermark/Stock Boston; pp.107, 118, 121: Rebus Inc.; p.110: Photofest; p.113: Museum of Political Life, University of Hartford.

Photo Research: Photosearch, Inc.
Cover art by Donald Christensen

The author would like to express her appreciation to Marcy Ross for her invaluable assistance in the preparation of this book.